"If you like hockey, and you like lau[...] like the writing of Sean McIndoe—o[...] Brown, as he refers to himself in the third person in airports and at weddings, for whatever reason—then I'm afraid you're really doing the math all wrong."

—*Bruce Arthur, National Post*

"DGB is the funniest hockey writer going—except for those times he makes fun of my brother. Then it's not funny. Okay, it's still funny."

—*Sean Pronger, former NHL player, www.jrnymnwear.com*

"There are a million guys trying to be funny, there are a million websites talking hockey, but Down Goes Brown does both without insulting the intelligence of the fan. That sounds easy enough; it's not. If it was, you'd have two million places to get it. Down Goes Brown is one of a select few who have been able to pull it off with both style and substance."

—*Tim Micallef, Sportsnet*

"The NHL isn't always known for its wonderful sense of humour. Hockey at the highest level is very serious business, and the quest for the Stanley Cup is no time for fun and games. That's where Sean McIndoe comes in. He always makes sure we don't take the National Hockey League, and ourselves for that matter, too seriously."

—*Jim Lang, The Fan 590*

"Down Goes Brown has a deft way of making fun of everyone in hockey, without actually offending anyone (most of the time). Whenever I am on the warpath about something, ready to blow, I read DGB, laugh, and calm right down. In the hockey world, he's one of a kind."

—*Allan Walsh, Player Agent, Octagon Hockey*

"In my opinion you would have to be sick in the head to be a Leafs fan—or at least have a sick sense of humour. I don't know about the former when it comes to Sean McIndoe, but he certainly has the latter part down pat. *Down Goes Brown* is one of the best hockey blogs out there when it comes to being what a blog should be—funny, irreverent, sometimes factual, and always a blast to read."

—*Dan Murphy, Sportsnet*

"Down Goes Brown is the best hockey humour writer in North America—and it's not even close. His jokes are guaranteed to make you laugh—even if your team happens to be the punch line."

—*Ian Mendes, Sportsnet*

THE BEST OF DOWN GOES BROWN

Greatest Hits and Brand New Classics-to-Be from Hockey's Most Hilarious Blog

by **SEAN McINDOE**

John Wiley & Sons Canada, Ltd.

For general information about our other products and services, please contact our Customer Care Department within the United States at (800) 762-2974, outside the United States at (317) 572-3993 or fax (317) 572-4002.

Wiley publishes in a variety of print and electronic formats and by print-on-demand. Some material included with standard print versions of this book may not be included in e-books or in print-on-demand. If this book refers to media such as a CD or DVD that is not included in the version you purchased, you may download this material at http://booksupport.wiley.com. For more information about Wiley products, visit www.wiley.com.

Library and Archives Canada Cataloguing in Publication
McIndoe, Sean
      The best of Down goes Brown : greatest hits and brand new classics-to-be from hockey's most hilarious blog / Sean McIndoe.

ISBN 978-1-11835-830-6 (print); 978-1-11835-842-9 (ebk); 978-1-11835-843-6 (ebk); 978-1-11835-844-3 (ebk)

      1. Hockey—Miscellanea. 2. Hockey—Humor. I. Title.
GV847.M33 2012   796.962   C2012-904134-3

Production Credits
Cover design: Adrian So
Cover image: Thinkstock/iStockphoto
Interior design and composition: Laserwords
Managing Editor: Alison Maclean
Production Editor: Lindsay Humphreys
Printer: Friesens Printing Ltd.

John Wiley & Sons Canada, Ltd.
6045 Freemont Blvd.
Mississauga, Ontario
L5R 4J3

Printed in Canada

1 2 3 4 5 FP 16 15 14 13 12

For Erica and Dougie

TABLE OF CONTENTS

FOREWORD

by Bob McKenzie

The Internet is a wonderful thing, and it looks like it's here to stay. This is mostly a good thing, but I must admit—with the advent of the information super highway, where virtually anyone can start their own website and "blog" to their heart's content, and the meteoric rise of social media outlets such as Twitter, where anyone, and I mean *anyone*, can have a "voice"—there have been occasions when I've seen or read certain things on ye olde Internet that suggest not every voice needs to be heard. But one of the voices from the wilds of cyberspace that does need to be heard, and has been heard, is that of Sean McIndoe.

Sean *who*?

Yeah, that was my first reaction, too. At first I thought the old Buffalo Brave NBA player had come back in the form of a wisecracking wordsmith with a passion for all things hockey . . . and the Toronto Maple Leafs. But that was Bob

(Two for) McAdoo, who I used to go watch when the Braves played some of their NBA games at Maple Leaf Gardens once upon a time.

You might know Sean McIndoe better as "Down Goes Brown." Or maybe not. Quick funny story for you in that regard.

I was in Ottawa for the 2011 NHL All-Star Game. One of my superiors at TSN—and I have many—mentioned that Sean McIndoe was dropping by for a visit. I probably should have asked, "Who the heck is Sean McIndoe?" but I'm like a lot of know-it-alls . . . when I don't know something, I'm not too quick to admit it. So I nodded knowingly and said, "Great."

Not long after that, a rather genial young man was introduced to me as Sean. We shook hands and made small talk—the kind where you say only enough so as not to reveal your total ignorance of who you're actually talking to. Afterwards I went on my merry way, though it was bothering me a little that I didn't really know who I had just met. So I went back to my superior—the Evil Quizmaster of *NHL on TSN* fame—and quizzed him as follows:

"Who was that Sean guy I just talked to?" I asked.

"Sean McIndoe," said the Evil Quizmaster.

"I know that," I replied. "But who is he?"

"Down Goes Brown," the Quizmaster said.

"Well, why didn't you say so?" I said. "Down Goes Brown, I know Down Goes Brown."

Fortunately, Sean McIndoe was still in the vicinity and I made some lame pretext to start up another conversation with him. This time I praised at great length some of his wonderful work as Down Goes Brown—a fairly lame and transparent effort by me to reconcile my previous lapse into oblivion.

Down Goes Brown is a very funny sonofagun. Sean McIndoe probably is as well.

I couldn't tell you exactly when I first heard of the blogger and diehard Maple Leaf fan living in Ottawa, which in and of itself is a ridiculously hilarious premise to begin with. Someone had been talking about Down Goes Brown, and I had the occasion to read something he wrote. I remember saying, "Hey, this is pretty good. This is funny."

Soon after that I was exposed to DGB's witticisms on Twitter, and I can attest there are few who make me smile or laugh more with a 140-character assault on the funny bone.

One of the good things about the Internet is that it subscribes to Darwinism, the old survival-of-the-fittest concept. Which is to say, it's one thing to have a "voice," but it's quite another to have something to say that enough people want to read on a consistent basis, making it worthwhile to keep writing. And it's that much more difficult if you're trying to be funny. Because funny ain't easy. Being funny is hard.

Down Goes Brown has passed that test, over and over and over again. He's funny, witty, sharp, self-deprecating, and he can write. This book you have in your hands is proof of all of that. So is his Twitter feed or his work on his website or in the *National Post* or on Grantland. It brings a tear to the eye—little Down Goes Brown is all growed up; he's moved out of his parents' basement (I don't actually know if his parents even have a basement, never mind whether he lived in it) and gone all "mainstream media" on us. Which doesn't really matter a bit, because if you do good work, where it appears is far less important than the quality. Do good work and people will find you. It's really that simple.

The piece Down Goes Brown wrote for his website on June 15, 2011—a game story recap published *before* the

Boston–Vancouver Game 7 of the Stanley Cup Final—is one of the most creative examples of writing I've seen. Turns out Down Goes Brown is not only funny, he's smart, too.

As for Sean McIndoe, well, I guess it's fair to say I wouldn't know him if I backed over him with my truck . . . I think I just opened the door for a Down Goes Brown piece on Bill Berg.

Enjoy.

FOREWORD

by James Duthie

"*The Best of Down Goes Brown* is a wild and whimsical ride through the world of sports through the eyes of one of the funniest and most creative writers of our generation."

—James Duthie,
multiple Gemini Award-winning host of
The NHL on TSN/best-selling author/
surprisingly chiseled physique

Editor: Uh, James? We asked you to write a foreword for this book, not a one-line quote. Oh, and by the way, if it were just a quote we wanted, we'd probably just use "The NHL on TSN Host" as your description.

Oh.

Well that bites. I always wanted to be one of those important-sounding guys on the back cover of books who use phrases like "whimsical ride." Now what the heck am I supposed to do? A full foreword? I mean, Down Goes Brown is freakin' hilarious and by far my favorite follow on

Twitter, but c'mon, who tries to pass off a collection of funny columns as an actual book?

Editor: Ahh . . . you did. Two years ago.

Crap. Damn you editors and your smartypants memories. Okay, I did write a book of sports columns. And some were kind of funny.*

But here's the thing. Back then, I didn't have much competition in the "Light-hearted-Sports-Columns-Mostly-about-Hockey-by-an-Ottawa-Guy-on-the-Internet" category.

Then Sean and his alter ego Down Goes Brown came along. I found him on Twitter, and he made me laugh out loud back when laughing out loud was something you really did, instead of an acronym you text someone after they text you something that isn't nearly funny enough to actually make you laugh out loud. DGB really will make you LOL until your BCOYN (Beer Comes Out Your Nose. . . . Yeah, I made that one up, but I think it might really catch on with the kids).

I'll admit I'm jealous of Sean now. I hardly have time to write anymore (TV boy trying to sound busy and important), and when I do, it's impossible to compete with his sick, demented (ultimate compliment words in my world) view of the sports world. Plus, now he's going to steal all my Funny Canadian Sports Column Book Groupies.**

The Best of Down Goes Brown is warped, whimsical (snuck it in . . . oh sweet victory), giddy fun from start to finish. This will be the funniest book you read this year. Hands down. (Unless you read the Swedish versions of the Stieg Larsson books . . . on Demerol after surgery.)

---

*If you read them really drunk. Or on Demerol after surgery.
**Okay, there was only one. Tanya in Montreal. Showed up for my signing looking for . . . heh . . . heh . . . heh . . . more than a book. (She had the date wrong. Thought it was a Jamie Oliver signing.)

ACKNOWLEDGMENTS

Thanks to my wife, Marcie, for her love and support, and for allowing me to watch hockey every single night for the last four years "because it's for work" without ever once pointing out that I watched hockey every single night for the twelve years before that too.

Thanks to my parents, Bob and Judi McIndoe, for believing I could be a writer someday even when I'd given up on the idea for the better part of a decade.

Thanks to my daughter Erica and my son Douglas, for being the two funniest people I've ever met.

Additional thanks to Bruce Arthur, Jim Bray, and Guy Spurrier at the *National Post*; to Bob McKenzie for being nice to people he does not recognize; and to the many others who have supported me in various ways over the course of this project, including James Duthie, Greg Wyshynski, Allan

Walsh, Katie Baker, Sean Pronger, Dan Murphy, Dave Naylor, Tim Micallef, Jim Lang, Jeff Marek, and Ian Mendes.

Thanks to Karen Milner, Lindsay Humphreys, Kim Rossetti, and Heather Ball at Wiley, and especially to my agent Brian Wood, whose heroic and tireless work on this project included inserting this line when I wasn't looking.

And finally, a special thank you to the readers who've been with me over the past five years as a completely unknown blog grew and grew until it became a mostly unknown blog. If you've ever posted a comment, clicked a Like button, retweeted a joke, or forwarded a link to a friend, you've helped me more than you know. My sincere thanks. I owe you a beer.

A COMPLETE TRANSCRIPT OF EVERY NHL GAME EVER BROADCAST

Voice-over: Welcome to tonight's coverage of every NHL game ever broadcast. Here's a montage of slow motion highlights set to non-threatening rock music. Now over to our in-studio host for tonight's game.

Host: Hello, everyone. I'm a little too excited to be here. With me is our panel of experts.

Management: I'm the former coach and/or front-office executive. Everything I say will be driven by grudges I still hold from my failed career.

Player: I'm the recently retired player. I'm still friends with most of these guys, so I'll never say anything interesting.

Media: And I'm the media guy. I will take every moment of the game and force it into a larger narrative for storytelling purposes.

Host: Who are you picking to win tonight?

Management: I'm picking the home team, because the visiting team fired me in 1983.

Player: I'm taking both teams, because I don't see why everyone can't be a winner.

Media: I'm taking the visitors, because I'm working on a story about concussions.

Host: Makes sense. Let's send it up to the play-by-play announcer and the analyst.

Play-by-play: Good evening. I'm a shameless homer, but will make a half-hearted attempt to disguise that if this is a national broadcast.

Analyst: And I will say things you already know, five seconds after you yell them at your television.

Play-by-play: We will now show you shots of both goaltenders, followed by a slow zoom on the referee with his hand in the air.

Analyst: Don't forget the shot of a coach staring into space.

Play-by-play: Something interesting has happened right off the bat, although you didn't see it because you were trying to read the line combinations that we flash on the screen in three-point font. Let's go down to the guy we've stuck between the benches. What did you think of that play?

Bench: I have no idea. You can't see anything down here and I'm terrified of being hit with a slap shot.

Play-by-play: Well, thanks anyway.

Bench: I will now go silent just in time for the players around me to teach your children some new swearwords.

Play-by-play: Very educational. Let's send it back to the panel for the first intermission show.

Host: Welcome to the first intermission show, where we ignore everything that's happened in the game so far and instead have the discussion we'd already prepared in advance. The home team has recently lost two games in a row. What fatal flaw would you randomly attribute those losses to?

Management: I'm going to say a complete lack of intelligence on the part of everyone who has ever been employed by the franchise.

Media: I'm going to attribute it to a lack of character, brought on by the disintegration of the traditional nuclear family.

Player: I'm going to chalk it up to small sample size.

Horrified silence.

Player: Just kidding. Let's go with character.

Host: Now over to the highlights guy, who is in the same studio but has to stand ten feet away from us for some reason.

Highlights: I resent you all terribly.

Host: Back to you guys in the booth!

Play-by-play: Welcome back. Here's a scoring chance . . . He scores! While we show you a close-up of a random defenseman in a passive-aggressive attempt to assign blame, let's bring in the former goaltender that we're legally obligated to include on every broadcast.

Ex-goalie: That one was totally not the goaltender's fault; it was deflected in off a stick.

Play-by-play: The goal came on a breakaway.

Ex-goalie: Exactly. The shooter deflected it into the net using his own stick.

Play-by-play: . . .

Ex-goalie: Those are the hardest kinds to stop.

Play-by-play: Have you ever seen a goal that was the goalie's fault?

Ex-goalie: Not yet, no.

Play-by-play: Let's send it back to the panel for the second intermission.

Host: When you last saw us, we were telling you how terrible the home team was. Now that they've had one good period, let's pretend that never happened and instead go overboard in praising how well they're playing.

Management: Here's a play from that last period, filmed from 15,000 feet above the ice. I will now scribble randomly on the screen with a Magic Marker.

Player: Everyone tried really hard on that play and seemed to have fun.

Media: Global warming!

Host: Highlights guy?

Highlights: (*sniffle*)

Host: Back to the action!

Play-by-play: It's a 1–0 game, which means you're in for twenty minutes of plodding defensive trapping that we'll pretend is entertaining.

Analyst: I will make vague references to a defensive "system" without ever explaining what that actually means.

Play-by-play: And now a fight has broken out. I will attempt to win a Gemini by pretending to be completely horrified.

Analyst: This is an overwrought comment about how nobody likes fighting, which you are unable to hear because the fans are cheering so loudly.

Play-by-play: And there's the final buzzer.

Analyst: This game went much faster than usual.

Play-by-play: Shut up.

Analyst: Here are tonight's three stars, which don't make any sense since we had to pick them with twelve minutes left in the second period.

Play-by-play: And now let's send it back to the studio for the post-game.

Host: Panel, before the game we all unanimously agreed that the home team would never win another game. Now that they've won, is it fair to say that it is in fact the visiting team that will never win again?

Management: Not unless they hire some new blood to the front office. Hint hint.

Player: I brought orange slices for everyone.

Media: Trapped miners!

Host: Highlights guy?

Highlights: Die. All of you.

Host: Thanks for watching, everyone. Stay tuned to watch anchors narrate highlights of the game you just saw!

2

THE TEN GREATEST COACHES IN NHL HISTORY

The life of an NHL coach is a tough one. Win, and the players get most of the credit. Lose, and the fingers always seem to point at you. And as fans of struggling teams know, the old adage "it's easier to fire the coach than the players" usually holds true.

But every now and then a coach emerges who manages to stick around long enough to craft a legacy. And those few who manage to win year after year, and sometimes even decade after decade, may eventually see themselves earn a place in the ranks of coaching immortality.

So let's pay tribute to some of those all-time greats. Here's a look at the ten winningest coaches in NHL history.

Scotty Bowman

Patented strategy: Would study the other team's roster carefully, then make sure that his had, like, a half-dozen more future hall-of-famers on it.

Possible weakness: Is pretty much the worst person in the entire world, according to people who've been stuck behind him going through an airport metal detector.

Career highlight: Achieved the ultimate goal in hockey on nine different occasions as a head coach; ten if you also count moving out of Buffalo.

Al Arbour

Patented strategy: Was known for emphasizing the importance of defensive zone positioning in practice. Specifically, "Don't position yourself too close to Billy Smith's crease if you like having two unbroken ankles."

Possible weakness: Retired in 1994 after devoting over twenty years to making the Islanders logo one of the most respected in all of sports, but forgot to remind the franchise not to replace it with a crazy bearded cartoon fisherman a year after he left.

Career highlight: His Islanders won nineteen straight playoff rounds from 1980 to 1984, setting a record that experts expect will remain unbroken until Gary Bettman has given out so many expansion teams that each year's playoffs are twenty rounds long.

Dick Irvin

Patented strategy: He strongly rejected accusations that his notoriously tough practices encouraged his players to use goon tactics, although he'd later admit that perhaps the linesman-punching drills ended up being a bad idea.

Possible weakness: Oh sure, he was supposed to be this legendary innovator, but when you try to get him to break down some simple game film on your iPad he's all, "Hey, how did you get this time machine into my living room? Get out before I call the police!"

Career highlight: Hockey fans around the world should thank him for rescuing the Canadiens from potential bankruptcy by turning the team around in the 1940s, since if he hadn't done that we wouldn't all get to laugh at what's happened to them now.

Pat Quinn

Patented strategy: Would keep the mood light at practice by having underperforming players take part in a fun drill called "Why don't you skate towards me as fast as you can and we'll pretend you're Bobby Orr."

Possible weakness: Often spoke of his open-door policy for players when it came to dealing with complaints about ice time, although he occasionally forgot to mention the part about that open door being attached to a cab that was on its way to the airport.

Career highlight: (Tie) Head coach of the 2002 Canadian Olympic team that united an entire nation by ending a fifty-year gold medal drought / Often managed to resist the urge to strangle Robert Reichel during games.

Mike Keenan

Patented strategy: While it's now become common for coaches to dictate specific matchups for their forward lines and defense pairing by constantly changing them on the fly, Keenan remains the only coach to use the strategy with his goaltenders.

Possible weakness: Was notorious for having personality conflicts with stars, which occasionally resulted

in reduced production from the player since every
slap shot they took during games was aimed at the
bench.

Career highlight: Won the Stanley Cup with the Rangers
in 1994, later admitting that he was so overwhelmed
with emotion during the final seconds of game seven
that he had to take a break from secretly negotiating his
new contract with the St. Louis Blues.

Ron Wilson

Patented strategy: Was among the first NHL coaches to
make extensive use of modern technology to formu-
late game strategy, although early in his career that
pretty much just meant deciding whether to use mostly
"fat guys" or "skinny guys."

Possible weakness: It's been said that players eventually
tune him out, although he argues that this reputation
is unfair because it doesn't take into account that blah
blah blah sorry I wasn't listening.

Career highlight: Guided the 2010 US Olympic team to
the biggest miracle on ice since 1980 when they managed to lose an important hockey game to Roberto
Luongo.

Bryan Murray

Patented strategy: His team meetings with the Senators
to go over strategy for that night's game would often
be interrupted by the confused former coach walking
into the room and saying, "Wait a second. Does this
mean I'm fired?"

Possible weakness: Only took his team past the second round of the playoffs once in his seventeen-year coaching career, although that's one more than Toe Blake ever managed and nobody complains about him.

Career highlight: Was instrumental in building the Anaheim Ducks into a contender as both coach and general manager, and they were so grateful they made sure he had a front row seat to enjoy their eventual Stanley Cup victory.

Jacques Lemaire

Patented strategy: Helped pioneer a trapping style in the mid-nineties that was imitated by virtually every team in the league over the next decade, according to your one friend who could actually manage to sit through any hockey games during that era.

Possible weakness: Devils players admit his "Hi, everyone, I'm the new coach" speech tends to get a little boring by the third time you hear it.

Career highlight: Won a Stanley Cup as coach of the Devils in 1995 after unveiling a complex new defensive system called "Oh hey, look, we have Martin Brodeur in net!"

Jacques Martin

Patented strategy: Would use a suffocating defensive system to lull his opponent to sleep, and then *BAM!*—here comes a slightly different suffocating defensive system.

Possible weakness: Preached discipline to his teams, but players report that behind closed doors he would sometimes respond to an especially tough loss by having a facial expression.

Career highlight: His five consecutive playoff series losses to the Maple Leafs is a modern-day record that experts agree is the most unbreakable in all of sports.

Joel Quenneville

Patented strategy: Coached the Blackhawks to a dramatic overtime win in game six of the 2010 Stanley Cup final using his famous "shoot the puck at the net and then jump around like you scored and hope nobody notices" play.

Possible weakness: His mustache kind of seems to have lost a step.

Career highlight: Beat the odds by becoming one of the few people ever drafted by Toronto to go on to a successful career in professional ice hockey.

3

THE OTHER FORMER NHL STARS WHO INTERVIEWED FOR COLIN CAMPBELL'S JOB

The NHL surprised fans during the 2011 off-season when they announced that controversial disciplinarian Colin Campbell would resign his post and be replaced by Brendan Shanahan.

Shanahan was a natural choice for the job, but sources tell me he wasn't the only candidate. It turns out that several other star players from Shanahan's era were also interviewed, and I've managed to obtain a top-secret transcript of the proceedings.

• • •

Scene: Gary Bettman's office.

Gary Bettman: Well, Brendan, that wraps up the interview. And I think Colin and I can agree that you completely nailed it.

Brendan Shanahan: Hey, thanks, guys.

Colin Campbell: You're a perfect fit for this job. But before we can make it official, we do have some other candidates to interview.

Bettman: Yeah, you know how it is. We need to make sure everyone gets a chance to speak with us. After all, you're not the only former NHL star who might be interested in the job.

Shanahan: Oh. OK, I guess that makes sense.

Bettman: Great, thanks for understanding. *(Into phone intercom)*: Send in Jeremy Roenick.

Voice on intercom: Right away, sir.

Jeremy Roenick: Hi, guys. Thanks for having me here. I really appreciate it.

Campbell: Thanks, Jeremy. My first question for you is—

Roenick: Nice desk. Is that mahogany? I love mahogany.

Campbell: That's great, Jeremy. If you let me finish my question, I was—

Roenick: You know back in 1991 with the Hawks, we were in a tough series with the North Stars . . .

Campbell: Stop talking.

Roenick: So I'm playing on a line with Steve Thomas, and it's late in the third period . . .

Campbell: Please stop talking.

Roenick: I'm afraid that's not possible. Once I get going I'm not physically capable of silence.

Campbell: Maybe we should move on.

Bettman: Good idea. Our next candidate is former Maple Leafs captain Wendel Clark. Why the interest in this job, Wendel?

Wendel Clark: Well, I'm really concerned about all the dirty hits these days. So I'd institute a strict policy to reduce them.

Campbell: Which is?

Clark: First offense, I punch you in the face.

Campbell: Wow. And on a second offense?

Clark *(cracking knuckles)*: There wouldn't be any second offenses.

Campbell: Good point.

Roenick *(still talking to himself)*: And then I say to Chelios, "Loosen up, old man, it's the nineties . . ."

Bettman: OK, our next former star is . . . uh-oh.

Wayne Gretzky: Hi, Gary!

Bettman: Oh man.

Campbell: Wayne, you're applying for my job?

Gretzky: Yeah, Colin. I'm looking to pick up some extra income. You see, my last employer didn't pay me everything they owed me.

Bettman: Um . . .

Campbell: What? That's an outrage! Tell me who it was, so Gary and I can go take care of it for you.

Bettman: Colie . . .

Campbell: I mean, this is hockey legend Wayne Gretzky. Anyone who would try to short-change him deserves a serious beatdown!

Bettman: Really not helping here, Colie.

Gretzky: Actually I don't think I'll need your help, because I brought a little backup of my own. I think you gentlemen remember *(pauses dramatically)* . . . Marty McSorley.

(Bettman and Campbell look behind Gretzky at an empty doorway.)

Gretzky *(confused)*: Marty? That's your cue, Marty.

(From outside comes the sound of tires squealing as a car makes a speedy getaway.)

Gretzky: I don't understand. Why would he take off instead of . . . oh. Hey, Wendel, didn't see you there.

Clark: Hello, Wayne.

Gretzky: I didn't know you were applying for this job.

Clark: Sure am. Want to hear my policy on uncalled high-sticks?

Gretzky *(sitting down quickly)*: No thank you.

Bettman: OK, let's just move on to the next candidate. *(Into intercom:)* Send him in, please.

Voice on intercom: Yes sir.

Patrick Roy: Bonjour!

Bettman and Campbell *(immediately)*: No.

Roy: Oh come on!

Campbell: Patrick, we saw you play. You were a crazy person.

Roy: So you don't want to hear about my "automatic suspension for turning down a goalie fight" idea?

Roenick: And then I deked past the twitching corpse of Sami Kapanen, went in and scored the overtime winner!

Clark (*leaning over to Roy*): Man, is that guy ever annoying.

Roy (*removing Stanley Cup rings from each ear*): What's that? I couldn't hear him.

Campbell: OK, so just to summarize: Wendel Clark wants to punch everyone in the face, Patrick Roy thinks goalie fights should be mandatory, and Jeremy Roenick couldn't run a suspension hearing because he wouldn't let anyone else talk. Also, Wayne Gretzky just high-sticked Gary Bettman in the face.

Gretzky (*holding bloody hockey stick*): Did not!

Campbell: Brendan, do you have anything to say about all this?

Shanahan: Um . . .

(*Everyone stares at Shanahan intently.*)

Shanahan: Hockey play?

Campbell: I knew you were perfect for this job. You're hired!

KNOW YOUR SPORTS
The NHL vs. the NFL

There's really no question about which league rules the sports world in the United States. With all due respect to the NBA, MLB and the NHL, there's just no stopping the NFL juggernaut. Thanks to billion-dollar TV contracts and wall-to-wall media coverage, the sport is simply unavoidable.

Well, if you can't beat 'em, join 'em. So even if you're a die-hard hockey fan, you may as well get to know a little bit about the world of the NFL. Here's a look at some of the similarities and differences between the two leagues.

NFL: "Safety" refers to a player who lines up deep in the secondary and is responsible for covering passing plays.
NHL: "Safety" refers to the act of not doing anything that might make Zdeno Chara angry.

NFL: If you see fans wearing cheese on their heads, you'll know that they are fans of the Green Bay Packers.
NHL: If you see fans with food on their heads, you'll know that whoever is throwing waffles at the Maple Leafs that night has a weak arm and poor depth perception.

NFL: Many players express their unique personalities by growing their hair long, sporting intricate tattoos, and performing choreographed celebrations after big plays.

NHL: Many players express their unique personalities by choosing a nickname that consists of their last name with the suffix "er" instead of their last name with the suffix "ie."

NFL: There are several teams in the southern United States that regularly play in front of sold-out crowds filled with rabid fans with a deep appreciation for the sport.

NHL: There are several teams in the southern United States.

NFL: You can buy commercial time during the Super Bowl, assuming you have a few million dollars sitting around that you'd like to waste on something that will have no discernible impact on your product's success.

NHL: Unfortunately, Ilya Bryzgalov doesn't hit free agency again until 2020.

NFL: Expect to see thousands of towels being waved madly by die-hard Steelers fans throughout the game.

NHL: Expect to see dozens of towels being thrown in by the Columbus Blue Jackets during the opening shift.

NFL: Teams will occasionally score from fifty or sixty yards away as the result of a play called the "Hail Mary."

NHL: Teams will occasionally score from fifty or sixty yards away as the result of a play called "playing against a team that employs Vesa Toskala."

NFL: If you see a player jump into the first row of the stands, it's because he's a Green Bay Packer and has just scored a touchdown.

NHL: If you see a player jump into the first row of the stands, it's because he didn't really appreciate that fan's most recent reference to his mother.

NFL: "The Music City Miracle" refers to a last-second kickoff return that allowed the Tennessee Titans to advance in the 2000 playoffs.

NHL: "The Music City Miracle" refers to an Ottawa Senators third-liner managing to marry Carrie Underwood.

NFL: A "dime back" refers to a sixth defensive back, who enters the game on likely passing downs.

NHL: A "dime back" refers to what you'd better be ready to give Patrick Kane once he's paid you for his cab ride.

NFL: Although they realize that it's probably unrealistic given the rate of injury, every player starts the season with the goal of playing in sixteen games.

NHL: Rick DiPietro.

NFL: "Bump and run" is a defensive technique that focuses on slowing down the receiver at the line of scrimmage.

NHL: "Bump and run" is Daniel Carcillo's strategy against any player who is tougher than Marian Gaborik.

5

A LOOK BACK AT GAME SEVEN OF THE 2011 STANLEY CUP FINAL

(which, due to a scheduling error, had to be published twelve hours early)

Author's note: Due to an unfortunate scheduling error that is too complicated to explain here, this analysis of the memorable game seven between the Vancouver Canucks and Boston Bruins ended up being published on my website twelve hours before the game was actually played. My sincere apologies for spoiling it for fans who had planned to watch the game that night.

So here we are. June 15, 2011. After a six-month season, four rounds of playoffs, and seven grueling games, the NHL has crowned its champion. The Stanley Cup has been awarded.

One fan base is devastated, while another will celebrate late into the night.

In the moments after a thrilling game seven, I'd like to address you directly, fans of the winning team.

It seems like only yesterday that your team was struggling through a first-round series against your bitter rivals who historically dominate you in the playoffs. But you survived, just barely, thanks to an overtime goal in game seven. Remember the excitement when the winning goal was scored, by that particular player? Little did we know the controversy that awaited them weeks later.

Your team waltzed through the second round against Peter Forsberg's old team, then beat that non-traditional, warm-weather franchise in the conference finals. And there you were, back in the Stanley Cup final for the first time in a generation. Who can forget that last time you played for Lord Stanley's mug, back in the early nineties? I bet you can still picture your team competing furiously, proudly representing those black and yellowish-gold uniforms that they wore then and perhaps still do, before finally going down to a bitter defeat. Damn you, Mark Messier!

But a generation later you were back, and this time the opportunity would not be wasted. It wasn't easy. It was a vicious series, in which your team persevered despite several sickening cheap shots by the opposing team. You endured your team being taunted with immature finger waves. You watched devastating hits on Nathan Horton and Mason Raymond, fifty percent of which you thought were unquestionably dirty. The entire hockey world outside of your particular city was united against your team, you told us, incessantly. And let's not even mention those shameless homer announcers on the other team's broadcast.

And then game seven. The series had seen it all, from overtime thrillers to lopsided blowouts to everything in between, and game seven certainly fit into one of those categories. All eyes were on Roberto Luongo. Many thought he would rise to the occasion while others thought he would crumble, and in the end we now know they were right. Without question, this game will be his defining legacy.

The end of the game must seem like a blur to you now. There was that goal scored by that one guy, and then that big hit with that other guy, then that other thing done by some other guy, and then the Conn Smythe won by Tim Thomas.

And then, the magic moment you'd been waiting on for four long decades, give or take a year. What fan among you will ever forget the sight of Gary Bettman passing the Stanley Cup into the waiting arms of good old number 33? And who says Europeans can't make great captains? Certainly not anyone who has had the pleasure of watching your team's leader, a truly unique talent. He certainly is one—or at the very most two—of a kind.

And now it's all over but the riot cleanup. Your boys are champions. A Stanley Cup banner will be raised in your arena next year. After an agonizing, debilitating, gut-wrenching test of your endurance as fans, it was all worth it.

But at least you're not like those fans of the other team. Imagine how devastated they must feel right now. Serves them right, those losers. Thank God you have nothing in common with them.

6

TAKE THE QUIZ

Do You Have a Concussion?

Concussions have been in the spotlight for several seasons now, as the NHL and its teams slowly but surely begin to take head injuries seriously. The league has even tried to standardize treatment by insisting that injured players undergo concussion-related medical testing prior to returning.

But fans may be surprised to learn that those "tests" aren't especially complex. They're actually just a simple one-page multiple-choice quiz, which has become the league's standard process for diagnosing concussions.

What does that quiz look like? Glad you asked, since I happen to have obtained a copy.

Dear NHL player:

You have recently suffered an injury, which resulted from a direct blow to the head. Congratulations! But before you can play again, league rules require you to pass the following in-depth test to ensure that you have not suffered a concussion.

Instructions: Answer each question and then add up your score. If you reach 100 points or more, you have a concussion and should not be playing; print out the results and show them to your coach.

1. **What's the last thing you remember thinking before you were injured?**
   - ❏ "I think I'll just cut across the blue line with my head down." (+5 points)
   - ❏ "What a nice pass I just made, I think I'll admire it." (+10 points)
   - ❏ "I'm pretty sure I can squeeze by Kronwall here . . ." (+20 points)
   - ❏ "Hey wait, why are the linesmen backing off and leaving me all alone with Milan Lucic?" (+30 points)
   - ❏ "I'll just adjust my rearview mirror and . . . how did Chris Pronger get into my backseat?" (+100 points)

2. **Which of the following common concussion symptoms have you been experiencing?**
   - ❏ Slight headache (+5 points)
   - ❏ Short-term memory loss (+10 points)
   - ❏ Nausea or vomiting (+20 points)
   - ❏ Starting to think that the Ilya Bryzgalov signing may have been a good idea (+50 points)
   - ❏ Really enjoying those NHL Guardian superhero things (+100 points)

3. **As a result of your injury, are you having any difficulty reading this test?**
   - ❏ I am experiencing significant difficulty. (+20 points)
   - ❏ I am experiencing minor difficulty. (+10 points)
   - ❏ I can understand everything I'm reading. (0 points)

❏ I can understand everything I'm reading, which is odd since I'm a European player who didn't speak a word of English prior to getting hit. (+100 points)

4. **At any point since being injured, have you experienced any of the following symptoms of double vision?**

❏ There appears to be 8,000 people at tonight's Islanders game, instead of the usual 4,000. (+10 points)

❏ In the family seating area, Philadelphia Flyers fans are furiously waving four middle fingers at my great-grandmother. (+15 points)

❏ During games in Columbus, there are twelve Blue Jacket players on the ice looking at their watches and mumbling about whether the season is over yet. (+20 points)

❏ Could swear that one of the Canucks keeps passing the puck back and forth with a guy who looks exactly like him. (−50 points)

5. **How did the fans react when you were hit?**

❏ Stunned into silence. (+5 points)

❏ Gasped in horror. (+10 points)

❏ Fight broke out in the upper level between fans trying to catch my mouthguard. (+20 points)

❏ Started throwing waffles at me, which made no sense. (0 points)

❏ Started throwing waffles at me, which made perfect sense. (+100 points)

6. **Has there been any media coverage of your injury?**

❏ A sports-talk radio caller briefly asked about it. (0 points)

❏ A TV report mentioned that I had suffered an upper body injury. (+5 points)

❏ A newspaper article speculated that I may have suffered a head injury. (+10 points)

❏ I was featured on an episode of HBO's 24/7 last night, which was subtitled *"The Ballad of Concussy McWobble'n'Fall."* (+100 points)

7. **Hey, just curious, but you do realize this is hockey and not soccer, right?**

❏ What? (+20 points)

❏ Sigh . . . yes. (−100 points)

8. **Finally, which of the following best describes your current role with your team?**

❏ I am a role player or fourth liner. (+20 points)

❏ I take a regular shift. (+10 points)

❏ I am a star player. (0 points)

❏ I am a star player and it is the playoffs. (Get out there, you're fine. Retake the test in the off-season if you still can't remember your name.)

7

THE CODE

Hockey's Unwritten Rules Revealed

Hockey fans often hear about the infamous "unwritten code" that governs fighting in the NHL. Any time there's an incident involving punches being thrown, you can count on someone making reference to The Code and whether a particular player's actions have violated it.

Unfortunately, it's a myth.

No, not the existence of The Code itself. It's the "unwritten" part that everyone has wrong. In reality, The Code has been written down in detail and passed on from one generation of NHL tough guys to the next. Every enforcer in the league has a copy; they just don't let us see it.

Until now, that is. I've obtained a tattered copy of The Code, and transcribed it below. It's time that hockey fans knew the truth.

Dear enforcer:

Welcome to the league. In your role as an NHL tough guy, you will be expected to conduct yourself according to a traditional set of rules and procedures. We call them The Code, and they are the rules we live by.

Please read The Code carefully and thoroughly, and follow it at all times.

Weight classes

All players shall be divided into the following weight classes, listed in descending order of toughness:

- Heavyweight
- Cruiserweight
- Middleweight
- Lightweight
- Doug Weight

Choosing an opponent

The Code dictates that players should stay within their weight class whenever possible. For example, a heavyweight may only fight:

- Another heavyweight.
- A cruiserweight who has instigated the confrontation.
- A lightweight who has attempted to injure a teammate.
- An overweight Flyers fan who has fallen into the penalty box.
- The nagging feeling that his job will no longer exist in three years.

Rules of engagement

Any of the following phrases, when spoken directly to an opponent, shall be taken as an invitation to fight:

- "Let's go."
- "Wanna drop the gloves?"
- "Would you like to hear a detailed rundown of my fantasy draft?"
- "Whoa oh, oh—this is Canada's team!"
- "I don't know, Paul. To be honest I find your Twitter account sort of juvenile and repetitive."

When to fight

It is considered appropriate to initiate a fight when:

- Your team has lost momentum at home, and you want to wake up the crowd.
- An opponent has committed a serious offense for which immediate retribution is required.
- Colin Campbell emailed you and told you to. (Note: It's probably a good idea to delete the email afterwards)
- You suddenly realize that you haven't been mentioned on *Coach's Corner* in almost three weeks.

When not to fight

Avoid fighting under inappropriate circumstances, such as when:

- The coach has given you specific instructions not to fight.

- Late in a close game, when an instigator penalty could result in a crucial power play.
- Your opponent is not expecting it, since he's busy listening to the national anthem.
- Some other completely inappropriate time, such as the playoffs.

Punishable acts

Any of the following acts shall be deemed in violation of The Code, and deserving of an immediate punch in the face:

- Shooting a puck towards the net after a whistle.
- Spraying snow on a goalie who has covered the puck.
- Attempting that cheap breakaway move from *NHL 94*.
- Being Sean Avery.

Removal of equipment

If, in the moments immediately preceding a fight, an opposing player:

- Removes his gloves: You must do the same.
- Removes his helmet and visor: You should do the same if you are given the opportunity.
- Removes his elbow pad: You may do the same if you so choose.
- Removes his shirt and pants: You should consider the possibility that you are not actually in a fight and have instead accidentally wandered into Patrick Kane's limousine.

When the fight is over

An altercation is considered over as soon as any of the following occurs:

- The linesmen make their first effort to intervene.
- One or both players fall to the ice.
- The opponent's trainer asks if you could hold off hitting him for a few seconds while they load him onto the stretcher.
- Pretty much as soon as it begins, if you are Matt Carkner and the other guy is Colton Orr.

This concludes The Code. Remember, memorize its rules and follow them at all times. (Unless, you know, somebody makes you really mad. Then just go ahead and do whatever you want.)

8

A MOMENT WITH THE GUY WHO HAS TO GO OUT AND FIX THE GLASS WHEN IT BREAKS

So then we ask for the manager, and he comes by the table and wants to know what the problem is, and we start telling him about how . . .

Wait. Everybody be quiet. Wait.

That last Dion Phaneuf slapshot off the end glass. It didn't sound right. No, I know it sounded fine to you, Jim, because you're new at this. But I know that sound. That's the sound of a pane of glass crying out. The ref is inspecting it now, but I already know what he's going to find. That glass is cracked, and that means the ref is going to turn and wave at us, and that means . . .

It's go time, team. *Go go go!*

Jim, Bill, Tom, you follow me. Somebody grab the ladder. Let's all awkwardly waddle-sprint across the ice and try not to think about how 18,000 fans are secretly hoping one of us will wipe out.

Waddle-sprint faster!

OK, we're here. Step one: Assess the damage. This one is bad, guys. We're going to need a brand new pane. What's that? Yes, Jim, we always need a brand new pane, every single time. But we still need to inspect it first to figure that out. Because that's the process, OK? Rookies.

Let's get set up, boys. Did we bring the right ladder? The one that's slightly too short for the job, and will force me to stretch in a way that reveals my belly button and makes everyone in the arena uncomfortable? Perfect. I'm going up.

All right, let's see here. Jim, I'm going to need you to bring me one of those little thingies that fits between the top of the glass. What do you mean, what's the technical name for it? That *is* the technical name: the little thingy that fits between the top of the glass. And no, I don't know what it's supposed to do, nobody does. It sits up there and then it occasionally falls out for no reason and stops the game. But we need to get one up there, stat, so I can whack it repeatedly with my hand until it fits. Go get one!

No rush. I'll self-consciously wait here on top of this ladder while everyone stares at me.

Ha ha. Well played, arena music guy. The *Jeopardy* theme—how very clever. Never heard that one before. Certainly very calming and helpful. Remind me to personally thank you the next time you come to me for help with a chipped windshield.

All right, Jim's back with the top of the glass thingy. Now let's remove the broken pane and replace it with a new one. Teamwork, everyone. Nice and easy. Good work. Bill and

Tom, you waddle-sprint the old pane to the back. Jim and I will handle the replacement.

OK, rookie, listen up. We need to lower the new pane in very carefully to make absolutely sure that it doesn't fit quite right. That's it—have it tilt off to the side just the slightest bit. Now everyone stare at it in confusion. More staring. Can you hear the crowd groaning? That's how you know we're doing it right. OK, back up the ladder I go.

Did you say something, fan sitting in the front row? I should "hurry up?" I am doing my best, sir. You don't think I'm aware that the entire building and a million people at home are all waiting for me? You don't think I know that the TV guys are making awkward conversation right now and showing random replays of things that happened three games ago? I'm well aware of the stakes here, sir. I hope nothing happens to slow me down, like one of my tools slipping out of my hand and landing on somebody's head in the front row. Could really do some damage, couldn't it? Any other helpful advice you'd like to offer? No, I didn't think so.

OK guys, one more trip up the ladder and I should have it. It's not quite in right but I'm pretty sure I can jam it down if I just sort of lean into it. No pressure. Everyone just stay professional. Nice and calm. Nice. And. Calm.

Stop staring at me, goalie! I am doing my best!

OK, I think we've got it. Let's blow this joint. Somebody grab the ladder. Waddle-sprint for the exit while we soak up the lukewarm smattering of applause, which is almost definitely intended to be sarcastic. We're almost home.

Phew. Great work, boys.

Yes, we have a thankless job. We don't get our name on the Cup. Nobody wants to interview us. Kids don't point at us and think about how cool it would be to have our job, like they do for Mr. Hotshot Zamboni Driver over there. And sure, every hockey video game has the glass breaking every three freaking minutes, but do they include a detailed mini-simulation where you take control of the guys who fix it? No, they do not.

But make no mistake, we are the unsung heroes of the NHL. And it's worth it. Because deep down, they need us. And we do our job with pride and professionalism, and at the end of the day that's all that matters. Because when it's all said and done, we can go home and look at ourselves in our slightly crooked mirrors, and we can know deep in our hearts that . . .

Wait.

Oh for the love of . . . *Dion, learn to hit the net!* Can't the coaches make him practice that or something?

It's go time boys. *Go go go!*

9

WHAT AN OFFICIAL NHL TRADE CALL REALLY SOUNDS LIKE

It's always exciting for fans when news of a trade breaks. These days, media often have the scoop on a transaction almost immediately, and quickly take to the airwaves or the web to share the news.

Fans may have noticed that these initial reports often allude to a deal being complete "pending a trade call with the league." The phrase brings to mind an intense conference call in which league officials grill the participants before grudgingly approving a deal.

But as it turns out, a trade call is simply a formality. And just like every other phone call you try to make these days, the entire thing is handled through an automated system.

Thanks to league sources, I got my hands on the top-secret number and gave it a call. Here's a transcript of what I heard.

Thank you for calling the National Hockey League. For service in English, press one. For service in French, press two. For service in whatever language Don Cherry is speaking, press three.

You have selected English. Please listen carefully, as our menu options have recently changed:

If you are a GM calling to complain about a penalty, press one.

If you are a GM calling to complain about a suspension, press two.

If you are a GM calling to complain about a goal review, press three.

If you are a GM calling to complain about having nothing to complain about, press four.

If you are an owner calling to report that you have recently gone bankrupt, press five.

If you are calling to report a completed trade, press six.

You have pressed six. You will now be connected to the NHL trade hotline. At any time, you may press zero to speak to Darren Dreger.

If you are trading away a draft pick, please enter the round number now.

You have chosen to trade a first-round draft pick. Is this pick lottery-protected in case you finish last? Press one for yes or two for no.

You have pressed two for no. Um, do you think that maybe you should rethink that? Press one for yes or two for no.

You have pressed two for no. Look, Brian, we've talked about this, wouldn't it make sense to at least ask if—

You have angrily mashed two for no.

Does your trade involve a player? Press one for yes, or two for no.

You have pressed one for yes. Please enter the line that the player plays on, and then his salary, followed by the pound key.

You have indicated that you are trading for a third-liner who makes $5 million. Are you drunk? Press one for yes, or two for no.

You have pressed two for no. Please indicate why you are making this clearly terrible trade:

> If you are trying to satisfy your idiot owner, press one.

> If you are trying to satisfy your idiot fans, press two.

> If you are trying to satisfy your idiot media, press three.

> If you've stopped caring because you're being fired at the end of the season and figure this will be the new guy's problem, press four.

> For all of the above, press five.

You have pressed five. Your trade is ready for processing. In a few moments it will be finalized, and you may inform the players and announce the deal publicly.

One last thing: Did you remember to check and see if the player has a no-trade clause? Press one for yes, or two for no.

You have drop-kicked your phone out an open window. Thank you for calling the NHL trade hotline. Goodbye.

THE SIGNS OF THE HOCKEY ZODIAC

A few years ago, astrologists briefly made headlines with a shocking claim: Thanks to a shift in the Earth's axis, we'd all need to learn new zodiac signs. Everyone was so stunned by the news that they spent days discussing the new system before eventually agreeing to forget it and just go back to the old one.

Did any of that matter to you? If you're a hockey fan, no, it didn't. That's because die-hard fans have long had their own unique set of astrological signs. Forget Scorpio and Capricorn; hockey fans have a better system that more closely aligns with the ups and downs of the NHL calendar.

On the off chance that you're a new fan or could use a quick refresher course, here's a rundown of the hockey world's zodiac signs.

Sign of the Opening Night (October): You're an optimistic spirit who chooses to see the best in people. You're willing to let the mistakes of the past stay in the past, and you believe that everyone deserves a fresh start. You know that you'll never be perfect, but you also understand that you can't obsess over every little thing.

Sign of the Long Season (November): You obsess over every little thing. You spend hours staring at yourself in the mirror, taking stock of every flaw and wondering how it's possible that you didn't notice them until now. You're haunted by a nagging sense that you were a fool for thinking things might actually work out for once. You probably drink too much.

Sign of the World Juniors (December): You're a shining example of the power of youthful exuberance. Emotional and excitable, you enjoy sprinting around and jumping into a wall whenever something goes well. You like to travel the world, even though everyone agrees that you'd probably be better off if you just stayed in Canada. You're really mean to Norwegian kids.

Sign of the All-Star (January): You're constantly reinventing yourself in an attempt to stay cool. Rich businessmen and small children love you, although everyone else finds you sort of tedious. Every time you hold a party, everyone spends weeks arguing about one or two friends that you forgot to invite. People often fake injuries to avoid you.

Sign of the Olympics (February): You're a world traveler who doesn't come around very often. Everybody loves you, even though you occasionally have an annoying habit of showing up at three in the morning. Whenever you attend an event that ends up being a huge success, you like to pretend you might not come back, even though nobody believes you.

Sign of the Trade Deadline (March): Everyone finds you endlessly fascinating, and people love to watch and analyze your every move in excruciating detail. Friends describe getting incredibly excited at the mere thought of your presence. But when you finally arrive, people are strangely underwhelmed and mutter, "Wait, I faked sick from work for that?"

Sign of the Stretch Run (April): Forget fun and games; you believe that it's time to get serious. You can be unpleasant and even downright cruel—and known to break a few hearts along the way—but nobody wants to be left off of your dance card. But deep down, you can't shake the feeling that everyone is using you to get to something better.

Sign of the Playoffs (May): You have a beard, and you enjoy shaking hands. You're intense and unpredictable, with exhilarating highs and excruciating lows. You can be almost unbearably difficult, but for those willing to persevere through the tough times, you offer the possibility of unmatched happiness that makes it all worth it. You never hang out with Maple Leafs fans.

Sign of the Draft (June): You're a long-term thinker who likes to plant seeds for the future and watch them grow. You have pimples, a bad haircut, a cheap suit, and a disturbingly gigantic neck; you absolutely will not put on a hat without bending it for five minutes first. You also don't hang out with Maple Leafs fans.

Sign of Free Agency (July): The good news: You're a shopaholic who loves the thrill of the hunt. The bad news: You usually make terrible financial decisions that will take you years to fix. Everyone warns you about this, of course, but you can't seem to help yourself. You would probably be a lot better off if you avoided talking with Russian people.

Sign of the Off-Season (August): You are incredibly dull and nobody likes you.

Sign of Training Camp (September): You are full of the inner peace that can only come with a new beginning, and you believe that a brighter future may be right around the corner. You trust in the power of youth and feel that all things are possible, even for people you just met. You embrace hope, dream big dreams, and eventually make the cutest little whimpering noise when reality comes along and mercilessly stomps holes in your soul.

11

THE NOT-SO-
ORIGINAL SIX

A Look Back at the NHL's
First Expansion Teams

Every hockey fan knows all about the Original Six. Even today, those six franchises dominate the game in terms of fan base and media coverage, and their rich histories make any matchup between them feel like something special.

But what about the *next* six? After all, the NHL added a half-dozen additional teams way back in 1967. While not all of them went on to the same level of success and prestige as their predecessors, surely those next six teams deserve to be just as well known and respected among the current generation of hockey fans.

Here's a historical look back at the NHL's Almost-But-Not-Quite-Original Six.

California Seals

Why they got a team: Satisfied the league's main criteria for a southern California franchise by agreeing not to name the team after a terrible movie.

All-time highlight: Impressively won the first two games in franchise history, although in hindsight celebrating that achievement by giving everyone the rest of the year off may have been a strategic mistake.

Lowest moment: Made a habit of infuriating fans by changing their uniform and color scheme almost every year with a series of increasingly amateurish designs, or as the NHL calls it these days, "marketing."

Lasting legacy: Eventually relocated to Cleveland, finished last for two straight years, and then folded. So basically, the most successful sports franchise in Cleveland history.

Minnesota North Stars

Why they got a team: Players occasionally complained that it got cold in Toronto and Montreal, and the league figured they might enjoy learning what that word actually means.

All-time highlight: Made appearances in the Stanley Cup final in 1981 and 1991, but were unable to win a championship due to their unfortunate insistence on adhering to the league's skate-in-the-crease rules.

Lowest moment: Were forced to move to Dallas in 1993 after Minnesota hockey fans sent a strong message that they would not support a professional hockey team that had a logo they could understand.

Lasting legacy: Taught us all that your dreams really can come true, assuming you are the 1988 Toronto Maple Leafs and your dream is to make the Norris Division playoffs with fifty-two points.

Pittsburgh Penguins

Why they got a team: The league knew that their new expansion teams could range from star-studded Stanley Cup winners to perpetually bankrupt disasters, and figured they'd kill two birds with one stone.

All-time highlight: Well, we could mention the back-to-back Stanley Cups, the brilliance of Mario Lemieux or Jaromir Jagr or Evgeni Malkin or Sidney Crosby, or the third Cup in 2009, but who's kidding who? It was when Jean-Claude Van Damme played a shift for them as goalie in the movie *Sudden Death*.

Lowest moment: Were widely accused of tanking the last few weeks of the 1983–84 season in an effort to draft Lemieux, which was unfair because their players showed a ton of hustle every night while repeatedly shooting the puck into their own net.

Lasting legacy: Have shown that even a smaller-market team can win a championship if they stay patient, develop a strong farm system, and remember to finish dead last whenever there's a generational superstar available in the draft.

St. Louis Blues

Why they got a team: Were awarded the last of the six expansion teams in a surprising decision over the consensus favorite, Baltimore, presumably after somebody in the NHL visited Baltimore.

All-time highlight: Played in the Stanley Cup final in each of their first three years after winning the all-expansion West Division, or as it was known back then, "The Division That Will Provide Cannon Fodder for the Actual Good Teams in the Final."

Lowest moment: Finished dead last in the NHL in the first season after the 2005 lockout after failing to bother signing any impact free agents, since every star player had sworn to never play in a league with a salary cap, and obviously nobody would lie about that sort of thing.

Lasting legacy: Made the playoffs for twenty-five straight years at one point, an era that included such memorable post-season moments as . . . um . . . that time they played that other team and then one of them won.

Philadelphia Flyers

Why they got a team: Because they said they wanted one. Do you have a problem with that?

All-time highlight: They became the first of the expansion teams to capture the Stanley Cup in 1974, although it's worth pointing out that they "captured" it by having Dave Schultz beat up all the security guards at the Hall of Fame and walk out with it.

Lowest moment: Wore full-length Cooperalls for a season, marking the only time in history that anyone looked at somebody from Philadelphia and wished they would take their pants off.

Lasting legacy: Apparently not much of one since they didn't even exist until the mid-90s, according to all these people who keep saying hockey is more violent now than ever before.

Los Angeles Kings

Why they got a team: The league had already decided to put the Seals in California, and apparently figured the state deserved a hockey team too.

All-time highlight: Beat Edmonton 6–5 in a 1982 playoff game that came to be known as the "Miracle on Manchester" because, younger fans assume, it featured the Oilers in a playoff game.

Lowest moment: Their blockbuster trade for Wayne Gretzky in 1988 paved the way for the NHL's aggressive expansion into the southern United States over the next decade, and look how well that turned out.

Lasting legacy: Performed an invaluable service to the hockey community by teaching a generation of young players an important lesson about how illegal stick blades are measured.

12

THE NHL'S TOP-SECRET FLOW CHART FOR HANDING OUT SUSPENSIONS

The NHL's suspension policy is a constant source of controversy. And whether it was former head disciplinarian Colin Campbell or current chief Brendan Shanahan making the call, you can always count on any decisions being criticized.

By now, fans are familiar with the refrain: Discipline is handed out haphazardly, almost randomly! There's no consistency! They're just making it up as they go along!

Nonsense. The criticism is unfair and unfounded. The NHL absolutely does have a clear policy about suspensions, and the policy is followed faithfully. The league just hasn't decided to share it publicly. So I'm doing it for them.

Yes, I have a copy of the NHL's discipline policy. And I think it's only fair that hockey fans everywhere get to see it. So here, straight from the league office, is the super top-secret policy for handing out suspensions:

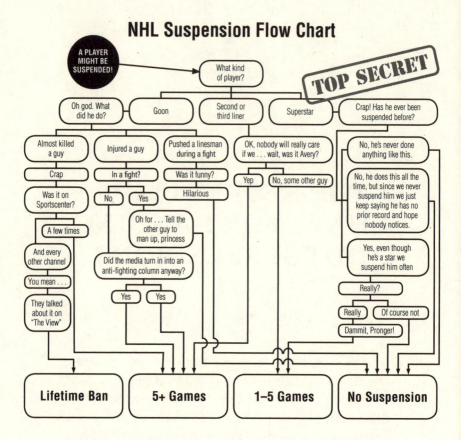

By the way, it should go without saying that this policy applies only in the regular season.

There's a separate policy for the post-season, which can be found here:

NHL Suspension Flow Chart (Post-season Version)

A PLAYER MIGHT BE SUSPENDED!

Is the other guy dead?

No

Yes

No Suspension

1 game

A BRIEF HISTORY OF MATS SUNDIN

Mats Sundin played for three teams during his eighteen-year NHL career. But for a generation of fans he'll always be a Maple Leaf, and in February of 2012 he saw his number 13 raised to the rafters in an emotional ceremony at the Air Canada Centre in Toronto.

Sundin's career was often spectacular, but his legacy is complicated. To this day, Maple Leafs fans can't seem to agree on what he meant to the team. He owns several franchise scoring records, but was criticized for underachieving. He refused an opportunity to leave the team, but was accused of lacking loyalty.

Now that Sundin has taken his place alongside Maple Leafs immortality, let's take a look back at the career of one of the game's most polarizing figures.

October 4, 1990: One year after being taken first overall by Quebec, Sundin makes his NHL debut in Hartford and records his first career goal in what, to this day, remains one of the most memorable moments in recent Nordiques/Whalers history.

June 28, 1994: A blockbuster trade sends Sundin to the Maple Leafs, with Wendel Clark going to the Nordiques. Upon witnessing the outrage in Toronto over the deal, Sundin makes a mental note that Leafs fans obviously really hate it when a popular veteran captain is traded for younger players.

September 30, 1997: Sundin is finally given the captain's "C" a full seven months after the Doug Gilmour trade had left it vacant, a delay caused by team president Ken Dryden's desire to "say just a few quick words" prior to the presentation.

January 7, 2004: The league suspends Sundin for one game after he tosses his broken stick into the lower bowl at the Air Canada Centre. The league argues that if it condones that sort of behavior, it could happen someday in a different arena and potentially endanger actual hockey fans.

May 4, 2004: Despite a dramatic tying goal from their captain late in the third period of game six, the Leafs suffer a series-ending overtime defeat to the Philadelphia Flyers. After the game, a disappointed but determined Sundin vows to never again lose another playoff game in Toronto.

February 26, 2006: Sundin plays a critical role in Sweden's upset gold medal victory at the Winter Olympics when he convinces Daniel Alfredsson to guarantee they'll win bronze.

October 14, 2006: Demonstrating his flair for the dramatic, Sundin scores his 500th career goal in overtime, while shorthanded, to complete a hat trick; although some fans will later point out that the accompanying unicycle and torch juggling may have been a little over the top.

October 11, 2007: Sundin sets two separate franchise records on the same play with a third-period goal that breaks Darryl Sittler's all-time marks for both goals and points; or, as the Toronto media will later describe it, "Sundin fails to break Sittler's single game scoring record."

February 24, 2008: While announcing his controversial decision not to waive his no-trade clause, an obviously conflicted Sundin tells reporters, "I cannot leave my team-mates and join another NHL club at this time." He then pauses, look around warily, and adds, "Soooo, if someone could tell Cliff Fletcher to stop honking the horn of the moving van in my driveway, that would be awesome."

December 18, 2008: After repeatedly vowing that he had no intention of playing half a season for a team and then winning the Stanley Cup, Sundin proves true to his word by signing with the Vancouver Canucks.

February 21, 2009: Sundin makes his return to Toronto and scores the winning goal in the shoot-out, giving Leafs fans one last chance to see him come through without any help from his wingers.

February 11, 2012: After watching his number rise to the rafters, and realizing that he should do something to acknowledge the outpouring of affection from Maple Leafs fans, Mats Sundin finally agrees to wave.

SIGNS YOUR CITY MAY NOT BE A VIABLE HOCKEY MARKET

When Gary Bettman became NHL commissioner in 1993, one of his mandates was to grow the game beyond its traditional markets. He set out to do that with an aggressive plan targeting the southern United States, and between expansion and relocations, the league soon found itself in several brand new markets.

The results have been mixed. While southern teams have certainly seen their share of success on the ice, most have struggled with the bottom line. The Phoenix Coyotes have been in a well-documented state of flux for a decade, the Atlanta Thrashers moved to Winnipeg, and teams in cities like Dallas and Nashville have struggled financially.

Some fans would conclude that the southern US just can't support NHL teams, but that seems unfair. After all, some southern markets do just fine. The key is figuring out which are viable hockey markets. And that can involve the league asking itself some tough questions.

Here are some signs that your local market may not actually be able to support an NHL franchise:

- When you try to describe the concept of icing to the fans by explaining that it's when the puck is shot all the way down to the other end of the ice, they respond, "That's great. What's 'ice'?"

- Any time they hear a fourth-line player described as "gritty," fans instinctively try to smother him in cheese and red-eye gravy.

- Nobody's coming right out and saying that the geographic location is too tropical for professional hockey, but "the wave" going around the arena right now is an actual wave.

- When their team goes on a power play, the fans just wait patiently for them to set up a scoring chance instead of instantly yelling "SHOOOOOOT" like real fans do.

- Scheduling has occasionally proven difficult since the arena is often booked for higher-profile events, such as rock concerts or NBA games or children's birthday parties.

- The fans in the new city never seem to grow attached to the team's logo and uniform colors, even though ownership has given plenty of chances by changing them to something new every six months.

- The kiss cam has recently been replaced by the "Let's see if we can find a section with more than one person sitting in it" cam.

- You throw your hat to celebrate a hat trick; by the time it hits the ice, it's riddled with bullet holes.

- The fans are always asking dumb questions like, "What exactly is the point of that trapezoid thing behind the net?" instead of just pretending to have any idea and then quickly changing the subject.

- As promised, the new arena that the city paid for immediately attracted dozens of new businesses to open up nearby, although it seems like a bad sign that every one of them is a moving company or a bankruptcy trustee.

- Instead of "Go team go!" or "Charge!" the most common fan chant is "Hey, could everyone out there on the ice keep it down? We're trying to catch the score of the college football game."

- When people come to visit your market they're always saying things like, "Gee, it's hot here" and "My, it's very warm even in winter" and "The name of this city is Phoenix."

- It's the first year in the new market and team management isn't even bothering to take basic steps to build a winner, such as calling up the Montreal Canadiens and asking if they want to give away their franchise goaltender for nothing.

- After the last home game of every season, the scoreboard flashes the message "To be continued?"

BEHIND THE SCENES AT THE REHEARSAL FOR THE PRESENTATION OF THE STANLEY CUP

OK, people, can I have your attention? Everyone listen up. You too, Mr. Bettman. This is important.

As you know, tonight's game marks the first time in this year's final that a team is one win away from taking the series. That means that the Stanley Cup will be in the building, and there's a chance it will be awarded after the game. It's a big moment, and we all need to be on the same page, so let's go over the game plan.

When the series ends, it's going to be chaos. Fans screaming, players hugging, linesmen stealing pucks. Everyone stay professional. And please, make sure the game is really done before you let the media storm onto the ice. Neither of these teams is the Buffalo Sabres, so it's important to try to actually get things right.

OK, once the handshakes are done the Cup will be brought out by the two guys who carry it everywhere: the guy who's never in any commercials and the guy who's in every commercial. Are they here? Great. You two will bring it out from the back hallway where it's been during the third period, being shown on television every fifteen seconds. Set it up on the little pedestal at center ice, and then go back to doing whatever it is you do the other 364 days of the year.

OK, Gary, once the Cup is out on the ice, that's your cue to make your way over. Let's walk through it right now. Great, great, you're here, one hand awkwardly on the Cup, ready to go. Pause for booing. Booing. More booing. Still booing. Hey, have you ever considered letting someone else handle this? It's just that the fans all really seem like they'd prefer it if . . . You know what, you're the boss. I'm not here to tell you how to do your job.

So anyways. . . Booing. More booing. Now, Gary, while all this is going on, you're going to want to be wearing the proper facial expression. I'd recommend a smirky mixture of glib condescension and bemused annoyance. Do you think you could . . . Hey, wow, that's really good. Have you been practicing?

Really? Permanent, you say? As in 24 hours a day? Hmm. Wow. OK, well, it's perfect, so don't change a thing.

So now some of the fans have given up on booing and are starting to hiss. That's a good time to start the presentation, so you're going to need to call over the captain of the winning team. Hold on, not yet. Wait until he's just started his interview with *Hockey Night in Canada*. And . . . now!

OK, Gary, remember this guy has literally spent the majority of his life focused on getting his hands on the Stanley Cup. He's bled for it, sacrificed, missed his children's birthdays, all for this one exact moment. So before you hand it over to him, make sure you force him to pose for photographs with you. He won't mind at all. That's right, be sure to hold the pose just long enough for it to feel awkward. Fantastic.

OK, now the winning team is going to pass the Cup around. There's an established order here, so let's make sure they follow it. First, the captain. Next, the sympathetic old guy on the team who's never won the Cup before. Next, any players who think they were unfairly singled out for criticism by fans and media. That should take care of the rest of the entire roster.

Now listen up, everyone, because once the players have the Stanley Cup we all have our most important job of the evening: We get out of the way. The NHL does a lot of things wrong, but this is the one moment we get exactly right. No owners grabbing the trophy. No corporate shills. No television personalities screaming into a microphone. Just twenty or so players who've endured two months of hell together, for this one chance to share the Cup. They've earned this. It's their moment. Let's all just stand back and absorb the positive energy.

Well, all of us except for Gary. The fans are still booing him.

Great smirk, though.

16

YOU WANNA GO?

A History of Hockey Brawls

Seen any good fights lately? Probably. While recent trends have shown a reduction in fighting, it's still part of the game. Usually it's just two players squaring off, settling their differences and moving on. But every now and then tempers boil over, everyone pairs off, and two teams get a little carried away.

Is fighting good for the game? Maybe not, but there's still nothing quite like a good old-fashioned hockey brawl to get a fan's attention. So join me in a nostalgic look back at some well-known hockey brawls. You know, or else I'll punch you in the head.

March 5, 2004: The Senators and Flyers combine for a league record 419 PIM after a series of fights are touched off by an argument over which franchise will destroy the careers of the most goaltenders during the rest of the decade.

October 2, 2008: After the fifth different altercation to feature a player viciously attacking Sean Avery, the Dallas Stars coaching staff decides to just cancel the rest of the practice and try again tomorrow.

April 20, 1984: The Canadiens and Nordiques combine for over 250 penalty minutes and ten ejections in a game that comes to be known as *la bataille du Vendredi saint* or, in English, "actually pretty standard for a game between Quebec and Montreal."

March 4, 2003: An enraged Darcy Tucker dives into the Ottawa bench and remains there for several seconds, inadvertently becoming the third longest-serving coach in Senators history.

1982 to 1993 (inclusive): In an extended incident that most hockey historians will later describe as "maybe a bit excessive," every single player in the Norris Division is involved in a spirited fight with every single other player at all times for twelve straight years, with the exception of Steve Yzerman.

March 15, 2006: Chris Pronger is ejected from the game after a rampage that leaves seven players injured, which is unfortunate since it was a spring-training game between the Baltimore Orioles and Kansas City Royals.

October 4, 2007: A rare goalie fight during an intrasquad scrimmage leaves Andrew Raycroft and Vesa Toskala facing significant injuries and lengthy suspensions, every Leaf fan really wishes in hindsight.

February 18, 1992: Towards the end of a wild bench-clearing brawl involving such noted enforcers as Rob Ray, Brad May, Gord Donnelly, Jay Wells, and Brad Miller, the Buffalo Sabres sheepishly begin to realize that the Hartford

Whalers left two hours ago and they've all just been fighting each other.

December 23, 1979: Mike Milbury climbs into the stands and beats a fan with his own shoe, in what everyone now agrees is probably the fifteenth or sixteenth dumbest thing he's ever done.

January 4, 1987: Canada and Russia are disqualified from the World Junior tournament after a massive brawl that will be unanimously criticized by the media as "outrageous" and "shameful" and "totally going to screw up the 'you never see any brawls in international hockey' argument we make in all our anti-fighting columns."

May 11, 1989: After an increasingly out-of-control Ron Hextall viciously attacks Chris Chelios in the dying moments of the Wales Conference final, concerned government authorities finally agree to green-light the top-secret cyborg assassin program that will eventually lead to the creation of Felix Potvin.

November 7, 1998: Red Wings and Avalanche players immediately engage in a half-dozen separate and bloody fights the moment the puck hits the ice, which really scares the crap out of the small disabled child doing the ceremonial puck drop.

FROM THE ARCHIVES

The 1993 Leafs/Kings
Game Six Live Blog

Author's note: This is a post from the DGB archives that was originally published in May 1993.

Wait, what? A blog archive from almost twenty years ago? That's right. A lot of you kids don't know this, but sports blogging has been around for a long time.

Long before the Internet even existed, die-hard sports fans like me were posting our thoughts for the world—it was just done a little bit differently than today. For example, back in the day we "blogged" by writing longhand in pen in a spiral notebook. If you wanted to add a photo, you cut one out of a magazine. When you were done, you "posted" your content by taping it to your front window. If other people liked your work, they would "link" to it by drawing an arrow pointing to your house and taping it to their own window.

Not many people noticed what you wrote, but occasionally somebody would wander by and read a few words. Then they'd usually roll their eyes, ring your doorbell, wait for you to open the door, and then drag you into the street to beat you up. So in that sense, not much has changed.

So let's travel back to one of the most famous games in NHL history. It's May 27, 1993, and the Toronto Maple Leafs are in Los Angeles to play the Kings in game six of the Western Conference final. The Leafs hold a 3–2 series lead and are one win away from meeting the Montreal Canadiens in the Stanley Cup final.

A young DGB, notebook in hand, was live blogging every moment. We'll pick up the action late in the third period, with the Leafs trailing 4–3.

1:38 a.m. Wow, is it ever late. I guess that's what happens when you've got a west coast game that doesn't start until 11:00 p.m. in the east. If this game goes to overtime I'm going to be completely exhausted tomorrow. I hope I'm not too sleepy for football practice, given my role as the star quarterback. I'd hate to disappoint my loving and devoted girlfriend, every member of the cheerleading squad.

1:40 a.m. Hey, still, these late games are way better than playing in the middle of the afternoon, am I right? Man. I don't know why NBA fans put up with that.

1:42 a.m. OK, back to the game. The Kings are still holding on to their one-goal lead. The Leafs look exhausted, which I suppose is to be expected. After winning two consecutive seven-game series, they're now playing their twentieth game in thirty-nine nights. It's a stretch of games that's literally unprecedented in NHL history, and you have to figure they're running on fumes.

It would have been nice for them to get some rest during this run, but then again, what's the league supposed to do—start taking a week off in the middle of the playoffs for no reason? Good luck sustaining any interest if you did that.

1:45 a.m. Leafs still trailing. I know I shouldn't look ahead, but I can't help but think we'd have a great chance against the Canadiens in the final. Don't get me wrong, the Habs are a great team and will no doubt be making regular appearances in the conference finals for years to come. But they've also been on an incredible streak of good luck— they've won an amazing *seven* straight OT games this postseason. Seven! There's simply no way that can continue in the next round.

I guess what I'm saying is I don't see the Habs beating either one of these teams in the final unless something miraculous happens.

1:46 a.m. Hey, totally off-topic, but have you noticed how Marty McSorley never seems to get any air under his shots? I have a friend who works on the Kings' equipment staff; I'm going to call him up after this series and suggest Marty start using a bigger curve on his stick.

1:48 a.m. Two minutes left. It's now or never for the Leafs. If they're going to make history tonight, somebody has to step up right now.

1:49 a.m. Felix Potvin stops a Kings 3-on-2 with ninety seconds left. He quickly plays it up to Gilmour, then heads for the bench. The Leafs are pressing as Wendel Clark hits the ice as the sixth attacker. Dougie finds him with a seeing-eye pass . . . and Wendel is all alone at the top of the circle!

1:49 a.m. Clark winds . . .

1:49 a.m. Clark shoots . . .

(Author's note: The notebook's next few pages are stuck together. Skipping ahead a bit.)

1:53 a.m. *(Extinguishes cigarette.)*

1:55 a.m. Wendel Clark is simply unstoppable tonight. That was his third goal, and they've all been beauties. This might be the greatest game of his career. It might be the greatest game of any Leaf's career, ever. He's single-handedly willing the Leafs into the final, and there's not a thing the Kings can do about it.

Mark my words: The Leafs are winning this game in overtime on their first even-strength shift.

1:57 a.m. Uh-oh. Glenn Anderson just drove Rob Blake headfirst into the end boards in the dying seconds of regulation. He got two minutes for boarding, and the Kings will start OT on the power play.

Now look, some Leaf fans are going to complain about a penalty being handed out this late in a crucial game. But I'm going to defend the referee, whoever that happens to be tonight. What Anderson did is a penalty. Period. It's right there in the rulebook. And you have to call it, even if it's an important game. Nay, you have to call it *because* it's an important game. The rules are the rules, and you can't ignore them just because you have to make an unpopular call.

1:58 a.m. Turns out the referee tonight is Kerry Fraser, by the way. Just making a note of it for the sake of completeness. I'm sure it won't end up being important.

2:00 a.m. And we're into the intermission.

2:10 a.m. Ugh. CBC is killing time before OT by showing us a bunch of Habs propaganda. They're doing features on some of their all-time greats. It's pretty standard stuff, although I did learn one thing: Did you know that former Habs tough guy John Ferguson has a son who took fifteen tries to graduate junior kindergarten? Inspiring story. I wish them all the best.

2:15 a.m. So nervous . . . We're one goal away from a trip to the Stanley Cup final. We just need to kill this penalty. Here goes nothing.

2:17 a.m. My God. Wayne Gretzky just high-sticked Doug Gilmour right in the face! Dougie is bleeding all over the ice. I don't have to tell you what that means: It's going to be five minutes and a game, since that's what the rulebook says and is how it's been called every single other time it's happened all year.

2:18 a.m. I mean, I really can't overstate how incredible this turn of events is. Wayne Gretzky is going to get kicked out of this game. They'll play four-on-four for a few more seconds, and then the Leafs will have an extended power play.

2:18 a.m. Look, not to get ahead of myself here, but good God almighty, the Leafs are going to score on this power play. There's no doubt in my mind. Wendel is unstoppable tonight. He's going to score, the Leafs are going to win the game, and then they're going to play the Montreal Canadiens for the Stanley Cup. I am literally seconds away from experiencing what will no doubt stand as the greatest moment of my young life.

2:19 a.m. Hmm, it's taking a lot longer than usual to call this penalty.

2:19 a.m. One more thought while they clear up whatever minor procedural matter is causing this delay. This high-sticking major on Wayne Gretzky, the announcement of which is no doubt a mere formality, is going to go down as one of the most stunning calls in NHL history. It will be discussed for decades. And Kerry Fraser is going to be the one to make it.

Imagine how he feels right now. With 20,000 fans in the building and millions more watching on TV, he's been handed a chance to make one of the toughest calls in league history. This is the moment that every official in every sport dreams of. This *exact moment* is why you pick up that whistle in the first place.

I guess what I'm trying to say is this: For the rest of hockey history, whenever you hear the phrase "Referee who stares down the biggest call of his career and chokes on his whistle," you will immediately think, "The exact opposite of Kerry Fraser."

2:20 a.m. Um, why is Wayne Gretzky taking the face-off?

2:20 a.m. WHY IS WAYNE GRETZKY TAKING THE FACE-OFF???

2:20 a.m. Oh God, he didn't call it. He didn't call it he didn't call it he didn't call it he didn't call it . . .

(Author's note: That goes on for several dozen pages. I'm just going to skip ahead.)

2:22 a.m. Hockey gods, can we talk?

Look, I understand what's happening here. Kerry Fraser just refused to call an obvious penalty that could have helped send the Leafs to a historic showdown with the Canadiens for the Stanley Cup. I see what you're doing, and I know where this is going. I know the Leafs are going to lose this game now. Every Leaf fan knows it. In fact, there's really no reason to string us along. You might as well just have the goal happen right now.

But first, just one request: Have it be somebody other than Gretzky who scores, OK? Anyone but the guy who still has Dougie's blood on his stick. That's not too much to ask, is it?

I'm so young and full of hope right now. My whole life as a hockey fan is spread out before me. So much optimism. So much possibility. And I can't help but feel like this could be a turning point, hockey gods. If you let Gretzky score right here, I'm going to have to go ahead and assume that you hate Leaf fans and want us to suffer forever. And I don't know if I could handle that.

But I do know this: I really don't want to turn into some bitter, burnt-out Leaf fan who rants about things that happened a generation ago in a way that starts off funny but gradually just makes everyone around him uncomfortable. Don't let that happen to me, hockey gods. Please. Just not Gretzky. Anyone but Gretzky.

2:23 a.m. Of course.

2:24 a.m. I will not cry. You will not get that satisfaction, hockey gods. Not tonight.

(Author's note: The next few entries are hard to read. I must have spilled a glass of water on them or something.)

2:32 a.m. You know what? This isn't the end of this series. Sure, it's a terrible way to lose. Sure, it will probably cost Kerry Fraser his career because even the zero-accountability NHL wouldn't try to defend this level of incompetence and will no doubt fire him first thing tomorrow morning.

But I'm not going to let this get me down. After all, I still have a lot going for me. The Blue Jays continue to dominate against smaller markets like Boston. Letterman's new show will debut soon and wipe Leno off the air for good. And *Chinese Democracy* should be out by the end of the year.

And most important of all: There's still game seven, Saturday night at the Gardens. The Leafs still have a shot. They may win. They may lose. But they still have a shot.

And I'll tell you this much: Wayne Gretzky just used up a lifetime's worth of luck tonight. If he's going to be a factor in game seven, he better be ready to play the best game of his career. Because if there's any justice left in the hockey world, his days of fluke goals are over.

Leafs in seven, baby. They're winning this series, and then they're beating the Habs. The dynasty begins now. The Maple Leafs are winning the Stanley Cup.

Because, man . . . God help me if they don't.

AN IN-DEPTH COMPARISON

Mario Lemieux vs. Patrick Roy

It's one of those wonderful coincidences that occasionally shows up in sports history: Two of the NHL's all-time greatest players, Mario Lemieux and Patrick Roy, were born just a short distance apart on the same day of the same year.

And while October 5, 1965, would go on to become one of the most famous birthdays in league history, it wasn't the only way in which the lives of these two hockey legends would overlap. Both players debuted in the 1984–85 season, both won multiple Stanley Cups, and both earned a spot in the Hall of Fame.

Of course, the two players weren't completely similar. Here are some of the subtle differences between two of hockey's most celebrated stars:

Roy: Often seemed to be the quickest player on the ice, despite playing the whole game wearing forty pounds of goaltending equipment.

Lemieux: Often seemed to be the quickest player on the ice, despite playing the whole game wearing 400 pounds of defensemen hanging off his back.

Lemieux: Was deceptively fast going from center ice to the goal, often arriving before the opponent's defense was ready for him.

Roy: Was deceptively fast going from the goal to center ice, often arriving before the Red Wings' goaltender was ready for him.

Roy: Was known to talk to his posts before an important game, even though he knew that they were inanimate objects that couldn't communicate back to him.

Lemieux: Occasionally hung out with the Samuelsson brothers.

Lemieux: The Penguins unveiled a statue in his honor in March 2012.

Roy: The Canadiens employed a statue as his backup goalie from 1990 to 1994.

Roy: Is one of the only players in hockey history to have had two different franchises retire his number.

Lemieux: Only ever had his number retired by the Penguins, although during the 1991 final he did leave Shawn Chambers's jockstrap hanging from the rafters.

Lemieux: Made one of the most famous plays of his career during the Olympic gold medal game in 2002, when he allowed an incoming puck to slide through his legs so that teammate Paul Kariya could score.

Roy: A few months later, paid tribute to Lemieux during game seven against the Red Wings by allowing incoming pucks to slide through his legs all game long.

Roy: Was caught winking at Kings' player Tomas Sandstrom during the Cup final because he knew with absolute certainty that he was going to win.

Lemieux: Was caught winking at Gary Bettman before the drawing at the 2005 Sidney Crosby draft lottery because he was being friendly. Why, what did you think it was?

Lemieux: Became inextricably linked with Wayne Gretzky at the 1987 Canada Cup when the two combined to score the winning goal in the final game.

Roy: Became inextricably linked with Wayne Gretzky at the 1998 Olympics when Marc Crawford apparently decided they were both equally qualified to take a shot in the shoot-out.

Roy: Put together one of the greatest clutch performances in post-season history in 1993 when he won a record eleven consecutive overtime games.

Lemieux: Has no idea what you're talking about, since he had the 1993 playoffs surgically erased from his memory.

Lemieux: Complained vocally about a 2011 Penguins/Islanders brawl because he felt the league had allowed the use of goon tactics to become too prevalent.

Roy: Complained vocally about a 2011 Penguins/Islanders brawl because he felt the goalie fight was way too short.

Roy: During a blowout loss against the Red Wings, had a heated conversation with the Canadiens team president that resulted in him being traded to the Colorado Avalanche.

Lemieux: Late in his career, had several heated conversations with the Penguins team president that resulted in his wife knocking on the bathroom door and telling him to stop talking to himself again.

Lemieux: Likely saved professional hockey in Pittsburgh in 1999 when he rescued the Penguins from bankruptcy and became their majority owner.

Roy: Has never been involved with ownership at the NHL level, unless you count Jeremy Roenick in the playoffs.

19

THE NHL'S PLAN FOR APPEALING TO VIDEO GAME FANS

At its heart, the NHL is in the entertainment business. And these days, that can be a tough business to be in. There's more competition for our attention and our dollars than ever before, and it's getting increasingly difficult to appeal to younger fans who may not have grown up with the game the way their parents and grandparents did.

The shifting interests of the younger generation, who increasingly prefer the quicker pace and instant gratification of video games, has become a league-wide problem. The NHL can't survive without the younger demographic, and right now that potential fan base often doesn't seem to like what it sees from the league.

Luckily, the NHL has a plan. Sources tell me that the league is already working on several initiatives to lure video game fans back to the NHL product. Here's the full list:

- Every game, one lucky fan gets to carjack the Zamboni and back over the driver.

- To make online gamers feel at home, replace traditional play-by-play announcers with racist and homophobic twelve-year-olds who apparently have no parents.

- Four words: Rock Band Brass Bonanza.

- Replace the shoot-out with an actual shoot-out.

- Stop referring to Maple Leafs penalty killers as "hesitant," "slow," or "lethargic." Begin referring to them as "laggy."

- During post-game interviews, encourage players to whine dramatically about the burden of avenging their dead fathers.

- All fights will now be preceded by a glass-breaking effect, for some reason.

- Players will no longer be suspended for touching off full-scale brawls by leaping off of the bench and charging wildly into a melee—as long as they remember to yell "Leeroy Jenkins" first.

- All games will now feature background music. Seven seconds of background music. Repeated over, and over, and over.

- At the end of every season, the Art Ross winner has thirty seconds to sign his initials on the high-score board.

- To make the television broadcasts look more like a sports video game, all fans will be encouraged to dress alike, be heavily pixelated, and constantly stand up and awkwardly wave their arms around for no reason.

- Bettman: Arkham City.

- Instead of a final buzzer, every game will now end with a brief cut-scene, classical music, and seventeen minutes of scrolling Japanese names.

- Hit the reset button on the entire league and reload the saved game from 1994.

A PERIOD-BY-PERIOD RECAP OF THE 2011 STANLEY CUP FINAL

The 2011 NHL season featured one of the best Stanley Cup finals in a generation. The matchup between the Boston Bruins and Vancouver Canucks featured everything a fan could want: heroes, villains, controversy, close games, blowouts, and of course, the stomach-churning drama of a deciding seventh game.

A series that memorable deserves more than just a game-by-game breakdown. So let's go one further, with a period-by-period review of the 2011 Stanley Cup final.

Game one: Canucks 1, Bruins 0

First period: In an effort to appeal to a younger demographic, the NHL announces that the role of the brooding but misunderstood vampire will be played by Alex Burrows.

Second period: As a neutral fan, you feel vaguely comfortable with the idea of one of these teams winning the Stanley Cup for the last time in the series.

Third period: Raffi Torres fools the Bruins' defense to score the game-winning goal by using a trick play he calls "Shoot the puck like a normal player instead of launching your elbow into somebody's temple."

Game two: Canucks 3, Bruins 2 (OT)

First period: Manny Malhotra makes an emotional return to the lineup wearing a full-face shield, which he will later admit is just an attempt to keep Brad Marchand from yapping in his ear all game.

Second period: In an embarrassing coincidence, the entire twenty-minute period is played without a whistle after all forty players simultaneously drop to the ice and roll around to draw a penalty.

Third period: The Canucks tie the game by scoring their third goal of the series, then quickly remind themselves to slow down and not use up the remaining five too quickly.

Overtime: Somewhere in the building, a Canuck fan who spent $2,000 on tickets returns to his seat eleven seconds late and asks, "So, did I miss anything?"

Game three: Bruins 8, Canucks 1

First period: Aaron Rome catches Nathan Horton admiring his pass and delivers a textbook open-ice check, but the anti-Canucks media go and make a big deal out of it being a "late hit" just because the pass was from the opening shift of game two.

Second period: The Bruins realize that since the Canucks are apparently planning to hit them late whenever they pass, it would be safer to just shoot the puck into the net every time they touch it.

Third period: In hindsight, Bruins coach Claude Julien admits he probably shouldn't have let Bill Belichick talk him into going for two.

Game four: Bruins 4, Canucks 0

First period: Bruins' legend Bobby Orr takes part in the pre-game ceremony, fires up the crowd, and then ruins the good vibe by asking if there's any chance he could be traded to Colorado.

Second period: The TD Gardens maintenance guy starts to worry that he really should have replaced the bulb in the goal light behind Luongo.

Third period: Frustrated Bruins players learn that their advanced scouting report on Canucks backup goalie Cory Schneider simply says, "Try to get a penalty shot and make his groin disintegrate so Luongo has to go back in."

Game five: Canucks 1, Bruins 0

First period: While sitting in his living room enjoying the series on TV, Tomas Kaberle gets the nagging feeling that he was supposed to be somewhere this month.

Second period: After demanding during a fiery intermission speech that the slumping Sedin brothers "look yourselves in the mirror" coach Alain Vigneault realizes that the dressing room doesn't actually have a mirror and the two brothers are just sitting across from each other staring creepily.

Third period: Roberto Luongo points out that Maxim Lapierre could never have scored that winning goal against him, in the sense that they're teammates.

Game six: Bruins 5, Canucks 2

First period: Bruins fans are widely criticized for mocking Mason Raymond as he lies on the ice with a fractured vertebra. But in fairness it's the first time they've accused an opponent of faking a broken back in, like, two months.

Second period: As he sits on the bench, an embarrassed Luongo begins to realize that the start times listed for the road games in this series are probably in Eastern time.

Third period: Bartenders in Boston start to wonder why customers keep trying to pay for drinks with bloody strips of green spandex.

Game seven: Bruins 4, Canucks 0

First period: The Bruins score the opening goal, but after a brief discussion NHL officials decide that they might as well go ahead and play the rest of the game anyway.

Second period: As the Bruins build an insurmountable lead, devastated Canuck players console themselves with the knowledge that at least they can still drive home in their luxury sports cars that they parked on the streets outside the arena.

Third period: As the closing seconds tick down, Ryan Kesler thinks ahead to which winner-take-all championship game in Vancouver he'd like to lose next.

KNOW YOUR SPORTS
The NHL vs. Soccer

Hockey fans typically experience severe withdrawal after the end of the NHL season. But this year, rather than sitting around all summer waiting on the occasional trade news and counting down the days to training camp, why not try something new?

For example, hockey and soccer are at least somewhat similar. Both are popular around the world, both involve trying to score into an opponent's net, and both combine the brilliance of individual stars with the strategy of intricate team systems.

But while hockey fans would no doubt appreciate the spectacle of the world's most popular sport, many don't understand it. Despite the similarities between the two sports there are also several differences, many of which are subtle and could prove confusing for novice fans.

That's why I put a call out to my various international bureaus, and we put together this guide to help hockey fans follow the "beautiful game."

Soccer: If you see a guy wearing flamboyant clothing who is struggling to communicate with you in English, he is likely a die-hard fan who has traveled from an exotic foreign land to attend the game.

Hockey: If you see a guy wearing flamboyant clothing who is struggling to communicate with you in English, he is likely Don Cherry.

Soccer: The sport is commonly called "football," although Americans often refer to it as "soccer."

Hockey: The sport is commonly called "hockey," although Americans often refer to it as "something to watch if there's no baseball, football, basketball, golf, NASCAR, poker, MMA, fishing, or bowling on TV."

Soccer: "Injury time" refers to the additional playing time added to the end of each half at the discretion of the referee.

Hockey: "Injury time" refers to lowering your head for a second when Raffi Torres is on the ice.

Soccer: Watching a game can be almost unbearable thanks to the *vuvuzela*, a South African noise-making horn that produces a horribly annoying noise that drones on nonstop for the entire game, leaving you fighting the urge to hurl the remote through your TV screen.

Hockey: Pierre McGuire.

Soccer: The games can start as early as 7:30 a.m., due to differences in international time zones.

Hockey: The games can start as early as 7:30 a.m., due to NBC not wanting to preempt any important infomercials or horse racing pre-game shows later that afternoon.

Soccer: In 1986, the "hand of God" sent Argentina into the World Cup semifinals at Mexico City.

Hockey: In 1993, the "hand of God" sent Marty McSorley's eyeball into the fifteenth row at Maple Leaf Gardens.

Soccer: A player will occasionally be granted a "penalty kick," presenting him with so much open net to shoot at that he's virtually guaranteed to score as long as he doesn't miss the net or hit the post.

Hockey: The equivalent is known as "shooting against Roberto Luongo in the playoffs."

Soccer: In an embarrassing display that any self-respecting sports fan would feel nauseated by, players will often react to even the slightest contact by pretending to be injured while rolling around pathetically on the grass.

Hockey: Completely different. The game is played on ice instead of grass.

Soccer: Riot police must often use tear gas, armored vehicles, and water cannons to subdue reckless perpetrators of violence known as "hooligans."

Hockey: Riot police must often use tear gas, armored vehicles, and water cannons to subdue reckless perpetrators of violence known as "the Boston Bruins."

Soccer: If you notice a player wearing a different jersey than his teammates, it's because he is the goalie.

Hockey: If you notice a player wearing a different jersey than his teammates, it's because he arrived five minutes late and his team had already done another jersey redesign.

Soccer: When a game is played under standard rules but won't have any actual impact on the final standings or eventual champion, it is known as a "friendly."

Hockey: When a game is played under standard rules but won't have any actual impact on the final standings or eventual champion, it is known as a "Maple Leafs regular season game after mid-November."

22

BEHIND THE SCENES AT AN NHL/ NHLPA COLLECTIVE BARGAINING SESSION

Scene: Summer, 2012. A large boardroom in a New York hotel. It's a fancy room, with oak-paneled walls, cathedral-style windows, and an ornate rotating fan spinning overhead. A handwritten sign taped to the door reads: "NHL/NHLPA Super-Secret Bargaining Session." On one side of the room sit various NHL players; on the other, several owners and team executives. Commissioner Gary Bettman and NHLPA head Donald Fehr share a podium at the front of the room.

Bettman: Can I have everyone's attention? I think it's time we get started.

Everyone settles into their seats and the room falls silent.

Bettman: OK, as we all know the current collective bargaining agreement is set to expire in September. Now, last time we had to negotiate a new CBA was back in 2004 and, it . . . uh . . . didn't go so well.

Grumbles in the audience.

Bettman: But that was then and this is now! And Donald and I both believe we can get a deal done if we can all get on the same page early.

Donald Fehr: I completely agree, Gary. We're here in the spirit of full cooperation, so let's roll up our sleeves and get to work!

Bettman: Great. OK, you know what, I'm having trouble seeing everyone. I think it would make more sense if maybe we moved that row of chairs over a bit so that we could all . . .

An angry murmur immediately spreads through the players.

Bettman: What? What did I say?

Brendan Shanahan *(stepping forward)*: Uh, moving things around like that could be considered realignment. You need the players' permission first.

Bettman: Oh for . . .

The players quickly huddle up around Donald Fehr.

Bettman: It was a simple common-sense suggestion.

The players return from their huddle.

Fehr: We think everything is just fine the way it is now.

Bettman *(sighing)*: No, it's not "just fine." Look, we have all the Winnipeg guys sitting out in the hallway. That doesn't even make sense.

Winnipeg players (*muffled, from the hallway*): Sure it does!

Fehr: Look, Gary, why don't you and the owners just move on to explaining your main issue with the current CBA?

Bettman: OK, sure. Basically, we need a system that will protect owners from runaway salary inflation that could potentially damage their team's viability.

Shanahan: Uh, Gary . . .

Bettman: Hold on, Brendan. Like I was saying, we need the players to help us create a system where overall spending is tightly controlled, and where we all—

Shanahan: Gary?

Bettman: Not now, I'm on a roll. The players need to understand that the current system makes it simply impossible for the owners to have any control over the . . .

Bettman pauses.

Bettman: Is something burning?

Shanahan nudges Bettman and directs his attention to the owners' side of the room, where a large bonfire is now burning on the floor.

Bettman: Is that . . . is that a big pile of money?

Owners: No!

Bettman stares disapprovingly.

Owners (*sheepishly*): Yes.

Bettman (*under his breath*)**:** Guys, we've talked about this. Why did you light a big pile of money on fire?

Sabres' owner Terry Pegula approaches, wearing a welding mask and holding a blowtorch.

Pegula: I don't know. All this talk of fiscal responsibility was getting kind of boring, so we all decided it would be fun to start setting our money on fire.

Bettman: All of you?

Pegula: Yeah. Well, except for the New Jersey guys. They're not having much luck.

Everyone looks over at the members of the Devils ownership group, who are unsuccessfully waving a lit match under a nickel.

Bettman: Wonderful.

Fehr: You see, Gary, this is the point we keep trying to make. The owners always want the players to make more concessions and agree to more restrictive rules, when all you guys need to do is just show some discipline and have each team stay within its means.

Bettman: It's not always that simple, Donald.

Fehr: It's not? Hey Olli, could you introduce yourself?

Olli Jokinen: Hi, my name is Olli Jokinen. I'm a borderline top-six forward who has never really lived up to expectations. I'm scheduled to be an unrestricted free agent this summer, so I'll be—

Jokinen is interrupted by the owners, who immediately start squealing and throwing wadded-up bills at him.

Fehr: See?

Bettman: OK, that's one example.

Fehr: Pavel?

Pavel Kubina: Hi, I'm a defenseman in his mid-thirties whose best years are well behind him. I was a healthy scratch in the playoffs, and I'll also be an unrestricted free agent if nobody—

Kubina is interrupted when a dump truck backs into the room and buries him under a pile of money.

Shea Weber: Wow, this is amazing!

Weber excitedly rushes to the front of the room.

Weber: Hi, everyone! I'm arguably the best defenseman in the entire league, and I'm still in my prime. I'll be a restricted free agent, so I can sign an offer sheet with absolutely anyone!

The room falls silent. A tumbleweed blows by.

Weber: OH, COME ON!

Bettman *(drumming his fingers innocently)*: Gosh, what an odd coincidence how that keeps happening.

Fehr: Yes, very odd.

Bettman: While we're at it, the owners are also demanding that we do something about long-term contracts. These front-loaded contracts for double-digit years have to end.

Fehr: What exactly is the issue with those deals?

Bettman: They circumvent the spirit of the salary cap, and what's worse, they upset competitive balance.

Paul Holmgrem *(leaping to his feet)*: Yeah! The Flyers were stuck with both Mike Richards and Jeff Carter on long-term deals, and we had to trade them both so we could finally try to contend for a championship!

Bettman: Um, Paul . . .

Holmgrem: I mean, how could you ever win anything when you're stuck with two guys like that?

Everyone stares at him uncomfortably.

Holmgrem *(eventually)*: I've been in the bathroom for three months. Did I miss anything?

Bettman: Um . . . we'll get you caught up later.

Holmgrem: Cool. By the way, the men's room is out of toilet paper.

Pegula *(producing a roll of thousand-dollar bills)*: I'll take care of it.

Fehr: Sorry, Gary, no deal. The players have to look out for their best interests.

Bettman: Well, Donald, the owners need to look out for our best interests.

Bettman and Fehr go nose-to-nose.

Fehr: Players!

Bettman: Owners!

Shanahan: Hey, does anyone else get the weird feeling that we're forgetting somebody in all of this?

Fehr: Players!

Bettman: Owners!

Shanahan: I just can't quite put my finger on it . . .

There's a sudden crash as the large rotating fan plummets to the floor in the center of the room.

Shanahan: Wow, that fan is just completely devastated!

Shanahan realizes that nobody else even noticed.

Shanahan: Um, guys?

The players are busy frolicking in the dump truck full of money. The owners are feeding the contents of their wallets into a shredder to see who can make the biggest pile. Bettman and Fehr, now wearing war paint, are circling each other menacingly.

Shanahan: Hmmm . . .

Shanahan stares at the fan. Or, to put it more accurately, the ex-fan.

Shanahan: Oh well, I'm sure it's not all that important.

OTHER COMPLAINTS ABOUT BRENDAN SHANAHAN

Brendan Shanahan may have the most thankless job in hockey. After an initial honeymoon period that faded quickly, the NHL's senior vice-president of player safety and hockey operations spent most of his first year on the job coming under heavy fire over his rulings on player discipline.

Don Cherry was one of the first to pile on the new sheriff, but he was hardly alone. Shanahan had plenty of critics in the media, reports indicated that some general managers were uncomfortable with his rulings, and plenty of fans voiced their concerns.

At the very least, you might assume that Shanahan's discipline decisions are the only area where he is feeling the heat. But you'd be wrong. According to my top-secret sources, the hockey world has a long list of issues and grievances with Shanahan that date back to the early days of his career.

Here's a sample of some of the hockey world's other complaints about Brendan Shanahan.

- In a cruel practical joke, spent his entire rookie year with the Devils whispering moronic coaching strategies into the ear of sleeping roommate John MacLean.

- Completely screwed up his shoot-out attempt at the Nagano Olympics when he failed to be Wayne Gretzky.

- Has been an NHL VP for almost two years now and has spent lots of time with Gary Bettman, yet has apparently still not taken him aside and convinced him to stop doing that "get overly defensive and make the whole press conference uncomfortable" thing.

- Whenever I get a penalty I don't agree with and then do the secret signal where I tug on my ear three times in the penalty box, the referee still has a job the next day. (Submitted by Gregory Campbell.)

- People are always going on and on about him having the second-most career goals by a left-winger, as if somebody's politics should be part of the story.

- He was supposed to be this noble tough guy who'd always stick up for a teammate, but when Claude Lemieux drilled Kris Draper into the boards from behind all he did was make excuses about how he "wasn't on the ice" and "didn't see the hit" and "was actually playing for the Hartford Whalers that year."

- He signed a very fair and reasonable contract with Glen Sather and the New York Rangers as an unrestricted free agent in 2006, so he's obviously the world's worst negotiator.

- Whenever you walk up to him and say, "Hey, nice belt, but I would have thought you'd be more into suspenders!" and then punch him playfully on the shoulder and laugh hysterically, he just stares at you like you're some kind of idiot.

- Oh sure, those videos he makes to explain his suspension decisions are nice, but how about dialing back the enthusiasm a little there, Mr. Electricity! *(Submitted by Sidney Crosby.)*

- He was traded straight up for both a young Chris Pronger and a young Scott Stevens at different points in his career, so who's really causing the head injuries around here, Brendan?

- Unlike the easygoing Colin Campbell, he's always hassling the IT guys with boring questions about whether there's a way to delete his old emails.

- Look, we all know "curse" is a strong word, so let's just say that every single team that ever traded him away mid-season ceased to exist within a year.

- He was drafted by the Devils and went on to play for the Rangers, and if there's one thing we know about guys like that it's that they end up being overpaid bums that ruin your salary cap for years, according to Habs fans.

- He was the second overall pick in the 1987 entry draft, so I'm not sure what you're talking about because I don't even remember him. *(Submitted by Alexandre Daigle.)*

- He was being completely reasonable and even-handed when he was suspending all those guys from other teams, but somehow became a complete idiot when he suspended a player from the team you like.

LEAFS VS. HABS

Hockey's Greatest Rivalry

The NHL has seen its share of rivalries over the years, but one looms above all the others: the Toronto Maple Leafs vs. the Montreal Canadiens.

The rivalry dates back almost a century and has seen the two teams capture thirty-five Stanley Cups between them. The Leafs and Habs have divided families, symbolized a culture, and helped to define an entire nation. From its earliest days during the NHL's infancy to the passionate heights of the fifties and sixties, through a lull in the eighties on to a rebirth in the nineties, the rivalry has produced a long list of memories.

Here's a look back at some of the most famous moments in one of sport's greatest rivalries.

December 26, 1917: Toronto wins the first-ever meeting between the two teams by a score of 7–5, thanks to a series of rookie mistakes by Canadiens defenseman Chris Chelios.

October 1, 1933: Legendary Canadiens goaltender George Hainsworth is traded to Toronto, where he'll go on to play every minute of every Maple Leafs game for three straight years. That feat won't be matched until the eighties, when every minute of every Maple Leafs game during the entire decade is played by "that freaking overpaid sieve with no glove hand," according to your dad.

July 1, 1946: Frank Selke takes over as general manager in Montreal after being forced out of the Maple Leafs front office due to a bitter and long-running feud with Conn Smythe, which oddly enough consists entirely of an argument over where their respective trophies should eventually be positioned on Steve Yzerman's mantel.

May 2, 1967: An aging and underdog Maple Leafs team stuns the Canadiens in six games to capture the Stanley Cup during Canada's centennial, creating a moment so dramatic and perfect that the organization immediately decides it would cheapen the memory to ever bother doing it again.

November 1, 1979: *The Hockey Sweater* by Roch Carrier is released and instantly becomes a beloved classic to an entire generation of young Canadians who understand how cruel other kids can be to children who dress better than they do.

November 7, 1987: The Maple Leafs trade speedy winger Russ Courtnall to the Canadiens for enforcer John Kordic, in a deal that fills the team's most glaring need: a player capable of repeatedly punching everybody who's going to spend the next few years complaining about trading Russ Courtnall for John Kordic.

May 29, 1992: Maple Leafs fans are initially skeptical of the hiring of former Canadiens coach Pat Burns due to concerns that he won't be able to communicate in their official language, before being reassured by Burns that he does indeed know how to curse at a TV screen while mumbling about next year.

June 13, 1993: On the one hundredth anniversary of the Stanley Cup, the Maple Leafs and Canadiens conclude what a generation of fans will fondly recall as the most thrilling and memorable final series of all time, in an alternate universe where Kerry Fraser bothers to read his rulebook.

October 5, 1996: Former Maple Leaf Vincent Damphousse debuts as captain of the Canadiens, and later admits that he finds Montreal's famed dressing room slogan, "To you from failing hands we throw the torch, be yours to hold it high," to be slightly more inspiring than the Harold Ballard–era Maple Leafs version, "Absolutely no refunds."

February 25, 1997: The Maple Leafs trade captain Doug Gilmour to the Devils, marking the start of a top-secret long-term plan known internally as "Operation Eventually Have Him Wind Up with the Canadiens So He Can Destroy Their Penalty Box."

May 30, 1997: The Maple Leafs officially name former Canadiens star Ken Dryden as the team's new president, after realizing it would be the only way to get him to stop answering the first question they asked him at the job interview three weeks ago.

January 27, 2002: Three former Maple Leafs—Doug Gilmour, Sergei Berezin, and Yanic Perreault—combine to score the historic 10,000th home ice goal in Canadiens history. The total does not include playoff or post-season goals, which would have seen the record reached years earlier, or intra-squad scrimmages, which would have seen the record reached three minutes into Andre Racicot's first practice.

April 7, 2007: In a thrilling game that features several lead changes and a furious Toronto comeback, the Maple Leafs eliminate the Canadiens from playoff contention in the final game of the season and earn the right to spend the rest of the summer figuring out which swearwords go best with "Wade Dubielewicz."

July 2, 2008: The Maple Leafs acquire center Mikhail Grabovski from Montreal for a draft pick, leaving the Toronto front office wondering why the Canadiens seemed so eager to move such a talented player, why the price wasn't much higher, and why Grabovski showed up with his pockets stuffed full of "Just FYI, Mike Komisarek is a free agent next year" highlight DVDs.

THE DETAILS OF DON CHERRY'S CONTRACT

It's quite possible that Don Cherry is the most popular media personality in hockey, but it's almost certain that he's the most controversial. In fact, Cherry is such a larger-than-life figure that even his contract negotiations can become headline news.

The pattern is familiar by now. Every few years we hear speculation that Cherry is on the way out. Inevitably, that's followed by word that he's signed on for another few years. The news thrills some fans, and infuriates others. And then we all move on.

Since this is hockey, any press release announcing a new deal always includes a line noting that "the terms of Mr. Cherry's contract were not disclosed." And while that may have been true initially, DGB spies were able to get their hands on a copy of the most recent agreement.

As you'd expect for a star of Cherry's stature, the deal includes a long list of special provisions and clauses:

- From now on, Cherry must agree to avoid the appearance of bias by being careful to refer to the Toronto

Maple Leafs as "they" instead of "we," such as in, "Boy, I really really really hope they win tonight."

- The deal is in the ten-to-twelve-million range, assuming we're talking jacket patterns.

- As in previous contracts, Cherry must pretend to understand Ron MacLean's show-closing pun at least twice per season.

- The deal has a no-trade clause, for reasons nobody quite understands, but we assume is related to that time the contract was left alone with John Ferguson Jr. for a few minutes.

- Cherry will have rights to use footage from the show in some sort of hockey-highlight video bearing his name, on the off chance he ever decides that's something he might want to do.

- The CBC agrees to continue to only employ stylists who don't know that goatees went out of fashion in 1996.

- Cherry will lead an annual seminar for all other former players and coaches in the broadcast industry entitled "A beginner's guide to having an actual opinion about something."

- In addition to *Hockey Night In Canada*, Cherry will be contractually obligated to make guest appearances on other hit Canadian television shows, such as . . . um . . . geez . . . is *Bumper Stumpers* still on the air?

- Cherry agrees to try to turn down the death metal rap that's always blaring from his dressing room by a few decibels, but he's not making any promises.

- *Coach's Corner* will continue to have a fake opening that just leads to another commercial, which will fool you into prematurely shushing everyone in the room and then feeling like an idiot every single freaking time.

- The contract will include a small raise for Cherry's support staff and administrative assistants, and a massive raise for the poor sap who has to do his closed captioning.

- The CBC agrees to assist in international efforts to track down every existing copy of the 1993 novelty single "Rock'em Sock'em Techno," load them onto a rocket ship, and shoot them into the center of the sun.

- Cherry will somehow continue to be allowed to be the only person on the planet to hold offensively outdated and moronic views, such as expressing a preference for his own country.

- In an effort to silence the chorus of critics who constantly demand that he be fired, each Cherry appearance will now be preceded by a brief reminder that he's just going to end up being replaced by Mike Milbury.

- Cherry will be limited to no more than five sick days per year, although Bruin fans know that he'll probably get confused and accidentally use six.

26

AN IN-DEPTH COMPARISON

Daniel Alfredsson vs. Zdeno Chara

Daniel Alfredsson and Zdeno Chara have a lot in common. Both are well-respected veterans. Both play in the Northeast Division. And both established themselves as stars while playing in Ottawa.

At the 2011 all-star weekend, they had something else in common: They each received the honor of being named as a team captain. That meant they got to draft the teams, choose the skills competition lineups, and lead the all-star squads that would bear their names. It also ensured that they're officially linked in the NHL's history books.

But while they share some characteristics, these are two very different players. Let's take a closer look at the two all-star captains.

Alfredsson: Born in 1972, on December 11.
Chara: Born in 1977, from March 13 to 18.

Chara: Has a wingspan of over seven feet if he spreads his arms out.

Alfredsson: Has a wingspan of over seven feet if we're counting his hairstyle from 2003.

Alfredsson: Once infuriated Maple Leafs fans by pretending that he might throw his stick into the stands before revealing that he was only kidding.

Chara: Continuously infuriates Maple Leafs fans by pretending that he might let Phil Kessel get a shot on goal that night before revealing that he's only kidding.

Chara: On several occasions over the years, has had to fight the other team's toughest players to send the message that his team can't be intimidated.

Alfredsson: On several occasions over the years, has had to fight the urge to grab the team's general manager and scream, "No, seriously, why don't you at least try getting us a half-decent goalie for once?"

Alfredsson: Is often referred to by teammates and opponents as "Alfie."

Chara: Is often referred to by teammates and opponents as "Whatever you want us to call you, just dear God please don't hurt anybody."

Chara: Was a guest at the unveiling of a statue in his likeness in his hometown of Trencin in honor of his greatest moment, his Stanley Cup win.

Alfredsson: Senators fans will probably present him with his own statue honoring his greatest moment, just as soon as they figure out how to sculpt a writhing Darcy Tucker onto the ground first.

Alfredsson: Has a deceptive skill set that can sometimes cause defenders to fail to realize how much speed he can generate until he's already blown by them.

Chara: Has a deceptive skill set that can sometimes cause team ownership to choose to spend all their money on re-signing a future minor leaguer instead.

Chara: Has the hardest slap shot in NHL history, according to the radar gun at the skills competition.

Alfredsson: Has a surprisingly decent slap shot himself, according to an angry Scott Niedermayer.

Alfredsson: His career has forced hockey fans to rethink their views on European players and their ability to serve as team leaders.

Chara: His career has forced hockey fans to rethink their views on slamming people's faces into metal stanchions, since most of us had assumed there was some sort of rule against it.

Chara: Is an avid cyclist who has occasionally ridden stages of the Tour de France course.

Alfredsson: Is an avid cyclist who has occasionally ridden stages of the Tour de Wait Why Are All the Senators Always Riding Stationary Bikes in Every Post-Game Interview?

Alfredsson: When he made his selections at the all-star draft, he was greeted with a warm ovation from an appreciative home crowd.

Chara: When he made his selections at the all-star draft, he was shouted down with loud boos, profanity and personal insults, although eventually the Canucks players quieted down and let him make his pick.

Chara: Is fluent in English, Slovak, Czech, Polish, German, Swedish, and Russian.

Alfredsson: Lives in Ottawa, so can presumably say, "The vegan restaurant is located between the shawarma place and the other shawarma place," in both official languages.

Alfredsson: No halfway competent general manager would ever trade him away.

Chara: No halfway competent general manager would ever trade him away.

TAKE THE QUIZ

How Will Your Team Do This Year?

The start of the season is one of the best times of the year to be a hockey fan. Training camp is done, final rosters have been announced, and the games finally matter again. Very soon, we get to start separating the contenders from the pretenders.

But what if you're the type of fan who doesn't like suspense? What if you can't be bothered to watch eighty-two games just to find out whether your favorite team will be any good this year?

You're in luck. By taking the quiz below, you can find out right now whether your team has what it takes to succeed. Simply grab a pen, circle the answer to each question that best applies to your team, and then consult the answer key at the end.

Spoiler alert: Don't read any further if you want to be surprised.

1. **What is your team's official marketing slogan for the coming season?**

   A) "Come and watch us on our quest for the Stanley Cup."

   B) "Win or lose, you'll always see an honest effort."

   C) "Hey, as long as everyone has fun and nobody gets hurt there's really no reason to keep score, right?"

   D) "Of course we have no chance, but at least the fans don't know that. Uh, remember not to write that last part down."

2. **During an exhibition game, you notice your team's coach is using one of those fancy new tablet computers behind the bench. When the camera zooms in on the screen, what would you expect to see him doing?**

   A) Drawing up a detailed play that's specific to the current personnel and game situation.

   B) Reviewing video of a play that took place earlier.

   C) Googling the phrase "How does 'icing' work?"

   D) Posting his résumé online.

3. **Your team's prized prospect is often referred to as:**

   A) Alexander Ovechkin without the mercy.

   B) Chris Pronger without the mean streak.

   C) Martin St. Louis without the size.

   D) Steve Mason without the limbs.

4. **Whenever experts discuss your team, what is the most common phrase they use?**

   A) "The presumptive Stanley Cup champions."

   B) "The dark horse contender."

C) "The complete and utter travesty of a team, an embarrassing collection of unskilled impostors, seemingly lacking in even the most basic human capacity for shame."

D) "The Edmonton Oilers."

5. **How often does your team take a "too many men on the ice" penalty?**

A) Never. The coaching staff has enforced an unshakable teamwide commitment to discipline.

B) Occasionally. But only because of confusion caused by those two all-star forwards being identical twins.

C) Often. Your players have difficulty with complex concepts, such as "six."

D) Never. The league has ruled that, due to their talent level, it is technically impossible for your team to ever be using "too many" players.

6. **When asked by a reporter for what he would like to be able to say about his team at the end of the season, the general manager replies:**

A) "That we won it all—nothing else will be acceptable."

B) "That we always gave it everything we had, even if it was in a losing cause."

C) "That we finished near the top of the league in ties."

D) "At the end of the season? You should probably ask somebody who'll still be employed here."

7. **Whenever you hear experts say that your team will contend for a championship, they immediately add:**

A) "Then again, I'm really just stating the obvious here."

B) "Of course, that's only if they're able to stay completely healthy."

   C) "This concludes my demonstration of the sort of thing people say when they've suffered severe head trauma."

   D) "e5."

8. **What is currently hanging from the ceiling in your team's dressing room?**

   A) A replica of last year's championship banner.

   B) An inspirational quote about never giving up during difficult times.

   C) Streamers, balloons, and a sign reading "Congratulations on winning a face-off."

   D) The starting goaltender.

Scoring: Total up your answers, then check below to find out how your team did.

Mostly As: Plan the parade!

Mostly Bs: Get ready to enjoy the ups and downs of an interesting season.

Mostly Cs: Oh well, at least you can look forward to a top-five draft pick next year.

Mostly Ds: . . . and every other year, forever.

BEHIND THE SCENES AT NHL REFEREE TRYOUTS

All right everyone, gather around. Welcome to day one of the training course to become an NHL referee. I'll be your instructor, and I'm going to teach you everything you need to know to earn your orange stripe.

I see we have a good turnout today. Wow, there must be hundreds of you. I can see why, of course. You're talking about a chance to be front and center in the greatest hockey league in the world. Who wouldn't want this job? Let's get started.

OK, everyone get in line and head out onto the ice. Once we're all out there, we'll . . . what's that? Yes, there are people in the stands booing you. Right, sure, one of them seems to be screaming horrible things about your mother. No, of course they don't know you and have never met you. What does that have to do with anything? Do you want to be a referee or not?

Hmm. Did a few of you just turn around and leave? That's weird. I guess they must have forgotten something in the locker room.

OK, let's get started by practicing some close calls down in the corner. Now, this is all going to happen really fast, so be ready. Get into the perfect position. Make sure you have a clear view. Watch carefully, and . . . make your call. Hey, look at all those hands in the air. Two minutes for hooking? Nice call. Go over and report it to the timekeeper. I'll admit that was a tough one, but hey, you have to learn to call it like you see it.

All right, we're just going to pause here for a moment so the broadcasters can analyze the play in super slow motion from ten different angles and explain to a few million viewers how you got it wrong. Just give them a minute. Don't worry, if your call went against the home team they'll show it on the giant scoreboard so everyone in the arena will get to see it too.

Let's run another play and see how you decide to call it. OK, this time I see that you decided not to call a penalty. Interesting. It was another close play, but if your judgment says it wasn't a penalty then that's absolutely what you should . . .

Oops, I heard a whistle. Oh look, apparently your partner at the other end of the rink decided to call a penalty on that play that happened right in front of you. That's right, the one you were standing five feet away from. He thinks you missed it. What's that? No, of course you can't overrule him. Why would we let you do that? No, you just stand there while he makes the call and basically tells everyone watching that he thinks you screwed up.

Hey, am I imagining things or did we lose a few more people? Weird.

OK, one last important thing to go over. In some cases a play may need to be reviewed, and you'll need to wait for the war room in Toronto to analyze the instant replay. What's that? How will you know when a review is taking place? Oh, we've taken care of that. You'll hear a special horn blast that will alert you. Let's listen to it now . . . there you go. Nice and loud. Hard to miss.

Is there a question in the back? Yes. Yes, that's right. You get to have a job where 20,000 people get to hear a special sound effect every time your supervisor thinks you may have made a mistake. Cool, eh?

OK, so you hear the horn and you skate over to the timekeeper's area. He'll hand you a phone through the hole in the glass. Try not to get the cord tangled. Yes, that's right, the cord. Because the phones are from 1972, that's why. Be careful with those things. They're valuable antiques.

I'm sorry, what was that? Why can't you just watch the replay yourself? Ha ha. Don't be silly. What kind of league would do that? Right, the NFL, exactly. What do they know?

OK, now it's time to announce the ruling to the crowd. Take a few steps back, face the camera, and look like you absolutely hate this part of your job. Now remember, when you're announcing the decision make sure you only actually say every third word. In the rare event that you've been given a microphone that actually works, you wouldn't want the fans to understand anything you were saying.

Let's all practice that. Perfect. You guys are really good. Well, the four of you who are still here. I could have sworn there were supposed to be more of you.

OK, so far you've been verbally assaulted by strangers, second-guessed by broadcasters, undermined by your colleague, and embarrassed by your boss. Hmm. We may not have time for the part where the players protest a call by wildly overacting because they know the game is being televised. We'll have to cover that tomorrow.

Well, congratulations, everyone. You made it through day one. We simulated a game, and you came through with flying colors. Now it's time to head back to the officials' dressing room, crack a cold beer, and reflect on a job well done. The game couldn't go on without you, and anyone who loves the sport owes you a debt of gratitude.

Hey, speaking of the fans, let's just see what they're saying about you on Twitter. There's some really well-thought-out feedback being shared here right now. This guy has a suggestion for you. Hmm. I didn't even know that was anatomically possible! You guys should really have a look at . . .

Guys?

Man, it's weird how that always keeps happening.

COME ON DOWN

A History of NHL Game Show Appearances

The NHL made an unexpected pop culture appearance back in 2010 when the Toronto Maple Leafs were the answer to the final question on the game show *Jeopardy!*

The question ("In action since 1917, this sports franchise is now largely owned by the Ontario Teachers' Pension Plan.") wasn't especially difficult. Two of the three contestants knew the correct answer, including Tom, the eventual champion. Hey, plan the parade, right?

But while it was certainly fun to see the Leafs make a cameo on one of the world's most popular game shows, it wasn't an especially rare sight. It may surprise younger fans to learn that the NHL actually has a long and distinguished history of showing up on some of television's most beloved games shows, albeit with mixed results.

Here are a few of the more memorable examples:

2008: After multiple attempts to explain the rules of the bidding portion of the game, exasperated producers for *The Price Is Right* are forced to disqualify Glen Sather after he is unable to grasp the concept of "without going over."

1994: While trying to figure out a way to get the blood and shards of teeth out of his hair, *Family Feud* host Richard Dawson vows to never again get lippy with the Sutter brothers.

1999: Despite following the proven formula of using a bland former lawyer as host, the NHL Network is disappointed by the negative critical reception and record low ratings for their production of *Win Gil Stein's Money*.

2004: During an uncomfortable episode of *Wheel of Fortune*, Gary Bettman spends twenty minutes squinting at a board reading "NOBODY IN PHOENIX ENJOYS WATCHING HOC-EY" without solving the puzzle.

1995: *The Hollywood Squares* becomes incredibly dull and ratings plummet during the years after special guests Jacques Lemaire and Lou Lamoriello develop a strategy that involves never doing anything except going for the block.

2005: An outraged Kyle Wellwood storms off the set of *Tic Tac Dough* after learning that he is playing for an assortment of cash and prizes, and not for actual Tic Tacs and dough.

2009: In a short-lived effort to appeal to hockey fans, NBC launches a show called *Deal or No Deal or To Be Honest I'd*

Love to Make a Deal But I Can't Do Anything Until the Trade Deadline Because of This Stupid Salary Cap.

2010: Lightning goaltender Dan Ellis declines an invitation to appear on *Who Wants To Be A Millionaire?* on the grounds that it would just end up creating more problems.

2007: A special "Enforcers of the NHL" edition of *The Weakest Link* unexpectedly turns out to be the series' final episode, although it does teach viewers a valuable lesson about what happens when you accidentally call Link Gaetz weak.

1984: Frustrated *Press Your Luck* host Peter Tomarken stops the show to explain to a St. Louis Blues fan contestant that while inconsistent goaltending is certainly an issue for any hockey team, there's still no need to punctuate every spin with cries of "No Wamsleys!"

2006: "NHL Arena Music Director" week on *Name That Tune* ends up being a disaster when none of them are able to name any tune that isn't "Welcome to the Jungle," "Cotton Eye Joe," or that one where they just keep saying "Woo-hoo."

1986: A young John Ferguson Jr. appears on *Let's Make a Deal*, trades a brand new car for a goat, and then immediately gives the goat a no-trade clause.

THE OFFICIAL MAP
OF AN NHL RINK

NHL fans learned something new during the 2011 playoffs: Colin Campbell revealed the existence of a "hitting zone" behind the net where, apparently, head shots are legal.

This got me wondering: What else don't we know about the NHL rink? So I dug into my old cartography library, and came up with this original map that lays it all out:

Official Map of an NHL Rink

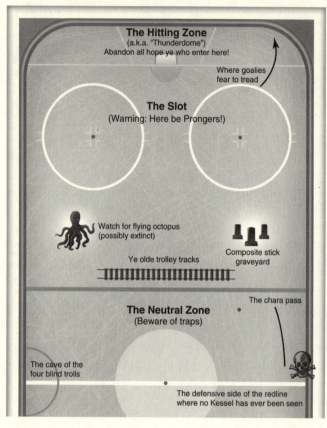

It all makes sense now . . .

31

A BRIEF HISTORY OF WAYNE GRETZKY

Hockey fans love a good debate. But ask them who the greatest player of all time is, and you typically won't get much of an argument: Wayne Gretzky will always be "The Great One."

From a playing career that saw him smash virtually every scoring record in existence to off-ice success behind the bench and in the front office, Gretzky has been a class act and an ambassador for hockey.

Let's take a look back at some of the highlights of his remarkable career:

January 26, 1979: On his eighteenth birthday, Gretzky signs a ten-year personal services contract with owner Peter Pocklington of the WHA's Edmonton Oilers. The deal makes Gretzky ineligible for that summer's NHL entry draft, marking the only known instance of the Oilers preventing a first overall pick.

December 30, 1981: Gretzky scores five goals against the Flyers, reaching the fifty-goal mark on the season in only

39 games to set a record that will surely be broken at some point in the future, assuming the league tweaks the rules to make each game three weeks long.

May 19, 1984: Gretzky wins his first Stanley Cup when the Oilers defeat a veteran Islanders team, causing a disappointed New York front office to acknowledge that it's probably time to get started on a quick thirty-year rebuilding plan.

July 17, 1988: After marrying Janet Jones in a million-dollar ceremony in Edmonton, Gretzky gets a bad feeling after noticing that every wedding gift from the Oilers' front office is luggage.

August 9, 1988: In one of the biggest trades in sports history, the Los Angeles Kings send Jimmy Carson, Martin Gelinas, three draft picks, and cash to the Oilers in exchange for Gretzky, Mike Krushelnyski, Marty McSorley, and a horribly awkward *Saturday Night Live* hosting spot to be named later.

October 15, 1989: Gretzky shows his flair for the dramatic when he breaks Gordie Howe's all-time scoring record with a goal in Edmonton, although some critics point out that doing it on a slap shot that first ricochets off Peter Pocklington's forehead in the owner's box seems like showing off.

February 25, 1991: Gretzky partners with Bruce McNall and John Candy to purchase the Toronto Argonauts, explaining that he wants to see what it would feel like to own a professional sports team besides the Calgary Flames.

May 19, 1993: Gretzky doesn't receive a penalty for high-sticking Toronto's Doug Gilmour in overtime, in an incident that your die-hard Maple Leafs fan friend admits he vaguely recalls hearing about way back when, before asking you to adjust the straps on his straightjacket.

February 27, 1996: Gretzky is traded to the St. Louis Blues and spends the next few months playing on a line with Brett Hull and scoring goals and getting assists and taking slap shots and . . . You know what? Nobody remembers this part of his career at all, so let's just move on.

July 21, 1996: Gretzky joins the New York Rangers as an unrestricted free agent, although he'll later admit he thought he was just signing up for a support group for people who recently had to endure the trauma of being coached by Mike Keenan.

April 18, 1999: Gretzky plays the last game of his career, waves to the crowd, then leaves the ice for the final time before turning to his teammates and saying, "Wait, why didn't anyone ever tell me I had one side of my jersey untucked this whole time?"

November 22, 1999: In unprecedented recognition of his remarkable career, the Hockey Hall of Fame is inducted into Wayne Gretzky.

February 18, 2002: Gretzky delivers his infamous Olympic rant in response to a question at a press conference, painting the Canadian team as the underdogs who the American fans and media are hoping to see fail. Gretzky later claims that the tirade was spontaneous, although many suspect the entire outburst was actually pre-planned, given that it came in response to the question "Um, excuse me, sir, but what are you doing at our luge press conference?"

November 22, 2003: Gretzky plays in his only old-timers event when he suits up for Edmonton in the Heritage Classic outdoor game, later admitting that he agreed to be surrounded by washed-up former Oilers one last time in an attempt to relive his years with the Rangers.

August 8, 2005: Gretzky is named head coach of the Phoenix Coyotes, and immediately reassures his players that even though he often scored over 200 points a season, he's pretty sure the team can still be competitive with the fourth liners only chipping in, like, 170.

February 12, 2010: As he slowly winds his way through the streets of Vancouver, Gretzky begins to wonder why the nice man who offered him a lift home from the Olympic Opening Ceremony insisted that he sit in the back seat of the pickup truck and hold a torch.

HOW TO SPEND
YOUR DAY WITH THE
STANLEY CUP

One of hockey's most beloved annual traditions is the sight of players from that year's champion team enjoying a day with the Cup, leading the trophy through a tour of small towns, big cities, and community barbeques. Each stop along the way is a feel-good story, as fans young and old get a rare chance to spend time with the greatest trophy in all of sports.

But while each player is given free rein to determine how to spend his day with the Cup, the league does provide some guidance. Each player receives a printed memo from the NHL head office with a few tips to help things run smoothly.

Most fans never get to see that memo, but I just happen to have come into possession of a copy, which I've reproduced below.

• • •

Congratulations on winning the Stanley Cup! As per hockey tradition, you are now entitled to spend one full day with the trophy in a location of your choice.

Before you plan your big day, however, the National Hockey League would like to offer several suggestions to help make your day more enjoyable:

- Consider having several small cards printed up that explain that the Stanley Cup is a trophy awarded to the NHL champion at the end of every season. This will save you from having to constantly stop and explain it to lifelong St. Louis Blues fans who have never seen it before.

- You're likely to meet fans who will want to take photos of their children or relatives sitting in the bowl of the Cup. For reference, the Cup can safely hold the weight of one large toddler, two small babies, or three Montreal Canadiens forwards.

- Remember that the Cup is made entirely of metal and is prone to tarnish if exposed to excessive moisture. Please keep it away from Jeremy Roenick, in case he starts bawling like a toddler again.

- The Stanley Cup is notable for its tradition of recording past champions with their names etched into the sides of the trophy. Given how easily the Cup can be scratched or dented, please respect the league's history by only dropping it so that it lands on forgotten teams such as the 2004 Tampa Bay Lightning or 2006 Carolina Hurricanes.

- When describing your Cup win as, "easily the greatest moment of my entire life," be sure to awkwardly add, "Um, other than my wedding day," if you think your wife may be listening.

- If you happen to meet an Ottawa Senators fan, he will want to tell you about all the Stanley Cups his team won back in the 1700s. As a representative of the National Hockey League, please do your best to listen to him politely for at least five full minutes before pulling the nearest fire alarm.

- The Stanley Cup is 117 years old. If you decide to take it to Denny's, don't forget that you can order off the seniors' menu.

- Impress your friends by pointing out that the engravings on the Stanley Cup include several typos and other errors. For example, in 1975 Bob Gainey's name is misspelled as "Gainy." In 1981, the New York Islanders are misspelled as "Ilanders." And in 1999, the Buffalo Sabres are misspelled as "Dallas Stars."

- Occasionally, a young child may ask you why the trophy doesn't list a champion for the 2004–05 season. The best way to answer this question is to ask the child for his allowance, use it to light an expensive cigar, and then blow smoke rings in the child's face while pointing and laughing.

- Please keep in mind that the Cup has been handled by literally thousands of players and fans over the years. Consider giving it a quick wipe-down with a wet paper towel before letting your newborn drink formula out of it.

33

DETERMINING WHETHER A GOAL SHOULD COUNT

The NHL War Room's Top-Secret Flow Chart

It's become a familiar scene over the years. A goal is scored, the defending team complains, the officials huddle up, and soon everyone is making their way over to the penalty box for a dramatic phone call. It's time to talk to the NHL's "war room" in Toronto, where various league officials will decide whether or not the goal should count.

But do fans really know what happens next? Sure, we all wait around, and eventually a decision is announced. But the actual review process is considered top secret. Fans have come to assume that the delay involves a rigorous review process in which league officials pore over every available angle, looking for even the slightest detail that could prove to be conclusive.

It turns out it's not quite that complicated. The NHL officials in the war room simply consult a simple flow chart that guides them through the various possible outcomes. And as luck would have it, I happen to have obtained a copy.

The NHL War Room's Top-Secret Flow Chart

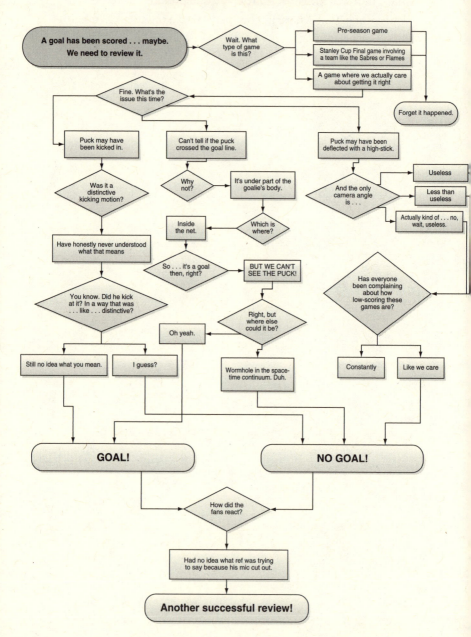

KNOW YOUR SPORTS
The NHL vs. MLB

October has often been called the best month on the sports calendar. For hockey fans, that's because the long off-season is finally over and the games that matter have started. But for other sports fans, October is special because of the baseball playoffs and the World Series.

Most hockey fans wouldn't dream of switching over to a baseball game after waiting all summer for the NHL season to start, but others are no doubt tempted to tune in knowing that a championship is on the line. So if you're a hockey fan who's thinking about checking out some action on the diamond, here's a handy guide to some of the subtle differences between the two sports to help you follow the action:

MLB: By late October, twenty-eight teams have already been eliminated from championship contention.
NHL: By late October, no teams have been eliminated from championship contention, with the exception of Edmonton.

MLB: Commissioner Bud Selig has been accused of having a conflict of interest in the games, since his family holds an ownership stake in the Milwaukee Brewers.

NHL: Commissioner Gary Bettman has never been accused of having any interest in the games at all.

MLB: "Blocking the plate" can get you seriously injured if you are a catcher and there is a close play at home.

NHL: "Blocking the plate" can get you seriously injured if you are dining with Dustin Byfuglien.

MLB: If you see the defense standing around helplessly while a player circles the bases before scoring, you'll know that batter has hit a home run.

NHL: If you see the defense standing around helplessly while a player circles the rink before scoring, you'll know that Steven Stamkos is playing.

MLB: It took the sport a generation to recover from the cancellation of the 1994 World Series due to a players' strike led by hard-line union head Donald Fehr.

NHL: I'm sure whoever's heading up the NHLPA these days would never do something like that.

MLB: In both 2010 and 2011, the Texas Rangers won their first two playoff rounds under the leadership of popular manager Ron Washington.

NHL: Nobody with "Washington" on their jersey ever wins two playoff rounds in the same season.

MLB: Outdoor games are sometimes cancelled due to rain.

NHL: Outdoor games are played even if it's raining, because come on, it's not like anybody is going to get hurt out there.

MLB: Both hands with palms down waved across the front of the body is the signal that the umpire has called a runner safe.

NHL: Both hands with palms down waved across the front of the body is the signal that it was a bad idea to try to fight Arron Asham.

MLB: A player who manages four different types of hits in the same game is said to have "hit for the cycle."

NHL: A player who manages four different hits in the same game is said to have "been scheduled for a hearing with Brendan Shanahan."

MLB: They call it the "foul pole," even though if the ball hits it, it's not actually foul. This is fascinating according to every single baseball fan ever.

NHL: They call it the "goal post," even though if the puck hits it, it's not actually a goal. Nobody cares because we have other things to talk about.

MLB: You can tell who gets to host game seven of the World Series by checking which league won that season's all-star game.

NHL: You can tell who gets to host game seven of the Stanley Cup final by checking which city's local businesses are hurriedly boarding up all their windows.

MLB: "Defensive indifference" refers to a play in which a runner is not credited with a stolen base because the defense did not make an effort to throw him out.

NHL: "Defensive indifference" is the title of last season's Toronto Maple Leafs highlight DVD.

MLB: Fans look forward to a mid-game tradition called the "seventh-inning stretch," in which everyone stands around and listens to a song from 1908.

NHL: Fans look forward to a mid-game tradition called *Coach's Corner*, in which everyone stands around and listens to opinions from 1908.

35

THE PROS AND CONS OF FIGHTING IN THE NHL

It's the oldest argument in hockey: Should the NHL crack down on fighting? The debate has spanned decades, filled thousands of newspapers pages, and dominated TV and radio broadcasts.

In recent years the stakes have gone up, as research into head injuries seems to suggest that fighting could contribute to long-term health problems in players. Combine that with the diminishing role of enforcers in the modern game, and some opponents of fighting feel the time is right to finally abolish it.

While the debate always leads to plenty of heated rhetoric, there's little evidence of anyone ever actually changing his mind on the topic. But maybe it doesn't have to be that way. I've spoken to experts on both sides of the issue, and I've captured their best arguments below.

For the first time, here are both sides of hockey's greatest debate presented side by side. Maybe, just maybe, we can settle this once and for all:

Pro-fighting: Banning fighting would eliminate the chance of a fight between Brad Marchand and Raffi Torres that the linesmen could just "forget" to break up.

Anti-fighting: Fights are nothing more than quasi-exciting but ultimately demeaning sideshows that don't showcase any actual hockey skills and have no place in the game—and these days we have the shoot-out for that.

Pro-fighting: Without the threat of fighting, noble enforcers like Arron Asham and Trevor Gillies would be unable to protect their teammates from despicable cheap-shot artists like Arron Asham and Trevor Gillies.

Anti-fighting: Let's face it, nobody really likes having fighting in the game except for ignorant know-nothings like fans, most general managers and coaches, and virtually every single player.

Pro-fighting: Getting rid of fighting would just result in every episode of *Coach's Corner* being nothing more than a seven-minute diatribe about no-touch icing.

Anti-fighting: If punching somebody in the face at a hockey game is outlawed, only outlaws will punch somebody in the face at a hockey game. And Flyer fans. Actually, mostly Flyer fans.

Pro-fighting: If we just hold off on doing anything to address the rapidly growing list of players lost to concussions for another year or two, all of us will eventually get to play in the NHL for a few games.

Anti-fighting: Fighting is an outdated concept that may have made sense for previous generations, but has no place in the modern game, like goalies playing without masks or an NHL team in Quebec City.

Pro-fighting: The inability to regularly write simplistic and condescending anti-fighting columns could spell the end of the already struggling newspaper industry.

Anti-fighting: Studies have shown that a total ban on fighting would increase hockey viewership by 20 percent in the southern United States, because Tom says he's pretty sure he'd start watching.

Pro-fighting: Hey, remember when they had fighting in *NHL 93* and then they took it out for *NHL 94*? Which one did you like better? Exactly.

Anti-fighting: In addition to being overpaid and overrated based on his Stanley Cup run, Niemi is known to snore loudly on team flights and often plays bad Finnish pop music on the Sharks' team stereo. *(Author's note: Wait, sorry, this should have been listed as an "Antti-fighting" argument.)*

Pro-fighting: Players engaging in fights face the possibility of devastating injury and even long-term disability, which is a risk that I as a fan sitting on my couch at home have decided I am willing to accept.

Anti-fighting: Eliminating fighting would send a strong message to impressionable children that settling a dispute by knocking somebody unconscious with your fists is unacceptable; instead, use your rock-solid shoulder pad like a gentleman would.

36

AN NHLer's GUIDE TO NEVER SAYING ANYTHING INTERESTING

If you're a National Hockey League personality, odds are you spend much of your day with a microphone in your face and somebody asking you a question. Many newcomers interpret this as an invitation to share their honest thoughts and opinions. It's not.

In fact, there are only a few dozen acceptable answers to any hockey-related question, and you'll be expected to simply choose the right one and recite it verbatim. Sure, some will accuse you of speaking in clichés, but it's better than the alternative: revealing yourself to have an actual personality, and being torn to shreds for it.

So for those of you who may be new to life in the NHL, here's a quick guide to the sort of things that are acceptable to say, and what you should avoid saying:

If you want to say: "Wow, a player on our team just committed a sickening act of violence for which he will surely be suspended."

Instead say: "I can't comment on that, since I haven't seen the replay."

But don't also say: "Because there was blood and bone fragments all over the scoreboard."

If you want to say: "Did we pay that guy too much? I think we paid that guy too much. Let me see the contract again. Oh man, we paid that guy *way* too much."

Instead say: "As per team policy, financial terms were not disclosed."

But don't also say: "Even though they'll be posted on CapGeek seven seconds after you read this."

If you want to say: "Sure, fighting Zdeno Chara sounds like a super idea!"

Instead say: "I think I'll just curl up in a little ball under my bench where it's safe."

But don't also say: "Hey, where'd this puddle come from?"

If you want to say: "Even though we're in last place and have lost seventeen games in a row, I'm not allowed to waive my no-trade clause because my wife says she really likes the shopping in this city."

Instead say: "I am absolutely committed to this team and want to win a championship here."

But don't also say: "Yes, honey, I was just . . . No, just talking to some reporters and . . . Yes, dear, of course, I'll be home immediately."

If you want to say: "This player is lazy, doesn't try hard, stops caring entirely for weeks at a time, and all his teammates want to strangle him."
Instead say: "This player is enigmatic."
But don't also say: "That's Russian for 'total head case,' right?"

If you want to say: "Our coach has been fired? Hallelujah! Now maybe we can all start trying again!"
Instead say: "It's always tough to see somebody lose his job."
But don't also say: "Now quick, somebody help me set his office on fire before they change their minds."

If you want to say: "I'm pretty sure that after that latest hit, our star player might be dead."
Instead say: "He is questionable to return after suffering an upper-body injury."
But don't also say: "In the sense that, technically, his upper body was the last-known location of his head."

If you want to say: "Hey, you know what would be fantastic? If my defensemen could go one shift without turning the puck over, screening me, and then deflecting slap shots past me. Can we maybe try that once, guys, just for a change?"

Instead say: "We win as a team, and we lose as a team."

But don't also say: "And after looking at this team, I've decided to go fight Brent Johnson."

If you want to say: "We are completely hopeless."

Instead say: "Hey, we just need a few bounces to go our way!"

But don't also say: "Like, if the other team's bus bounced off of the overpass on the way to the game, we could probably pick up a point."

DEMOCRACY DOESN'T WORK

A History of All-Star Voting

The NHL has allowed fans to vote their favorite players into the All-Star Game since 1986, and the results always give us plenty to talk about. It's become expected that fans will stuff the ballot boxes, start write-in campaigns for unlikely players, and generally look for ways to make sure the final results contain a surprise or two.

Debating the All-Star votes has become an annual tradition that dates back to the inception of fan-chosen teams. Here's a look back at some of the more memorable moments in fan voting over the years:

November 2008: Montreal Canadiens fans launch a ballot-stuffing campaign they discreetly refer to as "Operation let's get a mediocre defenseman elected to the All-Star team and then see if the Maple Leafs will massively over-pay him in free agency."

December 2006: The NHL scoffs at accusations that high-ranking league officials may have tampered with the results of the balloting, after announcing that a record 100 percent of fans voted for Gregory Campbell.

January 1987: Despite your careful efforts to punch the ballot just right and then hand it to the patiently waiting usher, you are devastated to learn that your childhood hero has not been selected for the game. Years later, you pinpoint the experience as the exact moment you learned the lifelong lesson that voting for things that are important to you is a complete waste of time.

February 2009: Three weeks after the All-Star game is played, mailed-in ballots from Blackhawks general manager Dale Tallon begin arriving at league headquarters.

January 1997: Claude Lemieux is flattered to learn that he has been named a starter on the Western Conference team thanks to a write-in campaign organized by Detroit Red Wings fans, although that feeling fades somewhat when he realizes that the same campaign has also elected Eastern Conference starters Rob Ray, Tie Domi, and an angry Doberman.

December 2008: Rick DiPietro casts a vote for himself, then spends six months on injured reserve due to the resulting paper cut.

January 2001: Defenseman Mark Eaton is the runaway vote leader in fan balloting, causing the league to rethink that season's heavily criticized "Delaware vs. The World" format.

December 2009: Attempts by Calgary ownership to encourage fans to flood the league office with write-in votes for

Flames players goes awry when the players mistakenly assume the slogan "This Year, Let's All Mail It In!" is the team's new mission statement.

January 2012: A concerted write-in campaign by Ottawa Senators fans results in the entire starting lineup consisting of variations of the phrase "Leafs suck."

December 2008: Sidney Crosby attempts to cast his vote, but is thwarted in his efforts to punch the ballot after being unable to locate its crotch.

October 1998: The NHL's first attempt at online voting proves unpopular with fans, mainly due to its requirement that fans log on to the website, click on their favorite player's name, and then mail their computer to the league's head office.

January 1991: Chris Nilan is named to the Wales Conference All-Star team by head coach Mike Milbury, which would be the funniest joke in this entire book except that it actually happened.

January 1993: The league's efforts to encourage grade school children to vote backfires when the two starting goaltending spots are won in a landslide by Ron Tugnutt and Daren Puppa.

TAKE THE QUIZ
Should You Rebuild?

To rebuild or not to rebuild? That's the question facing several teams every year. And while fans and media often talk about the decision like it should be easy, it's actually one of the toughest calls for a front office to make.

After all, if you start the process too early, you could miss out on a chance for one last run. And if you start too late, you may find your assets have lost their value. Either way, making the wrong decision could literally set a franchise back years.

If you're an NHL general manager and you're wondering whether the time is right to blow up your roster and start over, take this handy quiz.

1. **What would you describe as the main reason that you're hesitating to declare a full-fledged rebuild?**
    A) Realistically speaking, we have no need to rebuild right now since the team is already winning.
    B) Strategically speaking, it may be better to hold off until the off-season when we won't feel pressured to make any rash decisions.

C) Financially speaking, we're not sure how ticket-buying fans would respond to a rebuild right now.

D) Grammatically speaking, we're pretty sure we'd need to have actually "built" something before we could rebuild it.

2. **You can tell a lot about the direction your franchise is headed by how the team's youth is developing. When you ask the youngest player on your roster what he thinks it takes to be a winner, he:**

A) Looks around the dressing room and says, "I just need to watch the way these guys prepare every day, and do what they do."

B) Mumbles some clichés about hard work and perseverance.

C) Shrugs his shoulder and says, "Playing a game against us sure seems to work."

D) Adjusts his hearing aid and yells, "Speak up, sonny!"

3. **Most teams don't begin a rebuild if they still have a chance at making the playoffs. Based on the current standings, your team will make the playoffs as long as:**

A) There isn't some sort of work stoppage, since you've already mathematically clinched your spot.

B) You can stay healthy and avoid prolonged slumps, since you have a solid lead.

C) There's a surprise mid-season realignment that for some reason puts you in your own conference.

D) The league starts giving bonus points for regulation losses too, but only to your team.

4. **Attempts to rebuild can sometimes be blocked by veteran players with no-trade clauses. Do you think your star players would consider being moved?**

   A) Players would be reluctant to leave, but would be willing to accept a trade if it was in the team's best interest because of how well they've been treated by the franchise.

   B) It wouldn't be an issue, as we've wisely ensured that we don't have any no-trade clauses on the roster.

   C) It wouldn't be an issue, as we've wisely ensured that we don't have any star players on the roster.

   D) Does scrawling "Get me out of here" on their no-trade clause, wrapping it around a rock and throwing it through my bedroom window every single morning count as waiving? Because if so, we're probably all set.

5. **A rebuild may be unnecessary if you already have a strong crop of prospects in the minor leagues. What would you consider to be the single-biggest issue with the current state of your farm system?**

   A) We have so many elite prospects that we struggle to find ice time for everyone.

   B) We have fewer top prospects than we'd like, since we've traded some away in exchange for some of the top-tier NHL players in our current lineup.

   C) Whenever we try to call up a prospect, he says, "No thanks, I'll stay down here in the AHL where I have a better chance at winning the Stanley Cup."

   D) We have no prospects because we heard you were supposed to trade all of them for rentals, although

come to think of it, that really seemed to confuse
the kid working the counter at Hertz.

6. **It's important to have the support of ownership before undergoing a change in strategy. What does your team's owner say when you mention that you'd like to rebuild for the long term?**

A) Expresses concern because the current roster is already so strong.

B) Assures you that you're free to do whatever you think is best because he has absolute confidence in your judgment.

C) Insists that he be allowed to run any potential trades by his most trusted advisor, the GM mode in *NHL 95*.

D) Mumbles, "Uh, yeah, long term," before going back to giving Bob Gainey a tour of your office.

Scoring: Tally up your answers and check below to see how you did.

Mostly As: Keep your team intact, since it sounds like it's one of the best in the entire league.

Mostly Bs: Stay patient, but be prepared to move quickly if the team's performance takes a turn for the worse.

Mostly Cs: Act quickly: Package your veteran players in an attempt to clear out salary cap space.

Mostly Ds: Act quickly. Package your personal belongings and stray office supplies in an attempt to clear out your desk.

Mostly scribbles in the margins of the initials "NTC" with little hearts drawn around them: Yes, you do need to rebuild, but it's too late, John—the Maple Leafs fired you in 2008.

A TALE OF TWO HOMECOMINGS

December 2, 2010, was a memorable night on the sports calendar due to an interesting scheduling coincidence. That was the night that former Cleveland Cavalier star LeBron James and former Senators sniper Dany Heatley both made their heavily hyped returns to the cities they'd abandoned.

James was the bigger story, of course. His decision to join the Miami Heat as a free agent had been front-page news around the world for months. But Heatley's situation had also created plenty of bad feelings in Ottawa and beyond. And the similarities didn't end there.

Here's a look at two of sports' most notable villains, who briefly shared a night in the spotlight thanks to the schedule makers:

LeBron James: His decision to leave may have been influenced by Cleveland's reputation as "mind-numbingly boring" and "soul-crushingly dull" and "completely and utterly devoid of anything even slightly resembling a pulse."

Dany Heatley: His decision to leave may have been influenced by Ottawa's reputation as "a great option for people who can't handle the excitement of Cleveland."

LeBron James: Once it was apparent he would be leaving, Cleveland was forced to reconsider the massive "We Are All Witness" banner that had dominated the downtown skyline since 2005.

Dany Heatley: Once it was apparent he would be leaving, Ottawa was forced to reconsider the "Stanley Cup Champion" banners Daniel Alfredsson has been pre-ordering prior to every season since 1999.

LeBron James: By moving to Miami to play second fiddle to Dwyane Wade, revealed himself to be an athlete so lacking in competitive fire that he'd be willing to passively ride another player's coattails to a championship.

Dany Heatley: By moving to San Jose to play second fiddle to Joe Thornton, revealed himself to be no such thing.

LeBron James: Die-hard Cavalier fans booed him mercilessly as soon as he stepped onto the court.

Dany Heatley: Die-hard Senator fans booed him mercilessly as soon as he accidentally blocked their view of Spartacat's hot dog gun.

LeBron James: Attempted to rehabilitate his image in commercials for the league's biggest corporate sponsor, Nike.

Dany Heatley: Attempted to rehabilitate his image in commercials for the league's biggest corporate sponsor, Frankie's Used Car Emporium in Skokie, Illinois.

LeBron James: Apparently based his preferred destination on such considerations as "How will this affect my endorsement opportunities?" and "How will the local tax laws impact my earnings?"

Dany Heatley: Apparently based his preferred destination on such considerations as "This place isn't Edmonton, right?" and "No seriously, you're absolutely positive it's not Edmonton?"

LeBron James: Along with Wade, made it a top priority to ensure that former Raptor power forward Chris Bosh would also sign a free agent deal in Miami.

Dany Heatley: Prefers to pick up his own coffee and dry cleaning.

LeBron James: Would famously make a handful of chalk disappear into thin air before every home game.

Dany Heatley: Would famously make $4 million of Eugene Melnyk's money disappear into thin air every Canada Day.

LeBron James: After only a few weeks in Miami, was briefly embroiled in controversy after he appeared to lower his shoulder and initiate physical contact with his own coach.

Dany Heatley: Has never been accused of initiating physical contact with anybody.

LeBron James: Helped lead Cleveland to the franchise's first and only appearance in the final in 2007.

Dany Heatley: Helped lead Ottawa to the franchise's first and only appearance in the final in 2007, although if you're talking to a Senators fan it's easier to just pretend that you think accomplishments by a different team with the same name from a hundred years ago still somehow count.

LeBron James: Explained his decision during an hour-long special broadcast on national television, outraging fans and media and doing significant damage to his well-crafted reputation.

Dany Heatley: Wisely avoided that scenario by never explaining his decision, to anyone, ever.

THE NHL'S
HALL OF FAME
APPLICATION FORM

The annual announcement of the latest Hall of Fame inductees is one of the most anticipated dates of the year. Within minutes of the official announcement, fans around the world are debating the choices and arguing for their favorite candidates. Who was snubbed? Who got the call but didn't deserve it? Who should have been in years before?

The actual selection process is shrouded in mystery, relying on a secretive committee that prefers its discussions remain confidential. But as you might expect, certain details always leak out. For example, did you know that the entire process actually begins with a basic application form?

It's true. And DGB spies were able to get their hands on a copy of the 2012 application.

As a player who has been retired for three years or more, you are eligible for inclusion in the Hockey Hall of Fame. Congratulations! However, induction to the Hall of Fame is reserved for only the sport's greatest legends. In order to help us determine whether you meet the Hall's strict standards, please fill out this application form outlining your case.

First name: _____

Last name: _____

Nickname the media called you in print: _____

Nickname the media called you behind your back: _____

1. **The teams that you played for can, in some cases, influence your chances of being inducted. Do any of the following situations apply to you?**

    ❏ Played for a team in a major media market, which may provide me with a slight advantage.

    ❏ Played almost my entire career for a team everybody claims to watch but nobody ever does, and am hoping I can get in under the Federko Exemption.

    ❏ Played for the Maple Leafs for a few weeks when I was in my forties, and am assuming we can just fast-track this whole thing.

    ❏ Played most of my career for the Vancouver Canucks, so come to think of it I'm probably wasting my time here, aren't I?

2. **Offensive totals are an important part of any Hall of Fame case. If your numbers are not as high as other players', explain why you feel you should still be considered.**

❏ Played in an era when scoring was lower than it was at other points in history.

❏ Shifted into a more defensive style of play later in my career.

❏ Was injured for a few games against Andrew Raycroft back in 2007, so probably missed out on thirty or forty more goals.

❏ Saw how much trouble Adam Oates was having getting in; just assumed you guys thought that scoring a ton of points was somehow a bad thing.

3. **Hall of Fame rules limit us to four player inductions per year. Are there any high-profile 2012 candidates that you think we should pass on this time?**

❏ Mats Sundin, since it would probably take him six months to decide whether or not he wants to attend the induction ceremony.

❏ Eric Lindros, since it would just be awkward for everyone when his plaque completely forgets that he once played for the Dallas Stars.

❏ Pavel Bure, since it would be fun to see how Canucks fans would figure out a way to blame it on the Bruins.

❏ Pat Burns, since he was obviously inducted unanimously when he was first eligible two years ago, and only appears on this year's ballot because of a typo, right?

4. **Winning one or more championships can certainly bolster your case. Do you have your name on the Stanley Cup?**

❏ Sorry, am having trouble checking an option since my hand is so weighed down by all these giant rings.

❏ Was a dedicated team player completely focused on reaching the ultimate goal of winning a championship, and finally achieved that late in my career by demanding that my loser franchise trade me to a way better team.

❏ Um, you saw the part up above where I mentioned playing for the Canucks, right?

❏ Didn't have my name on the Cup when I first came by the Hall of Fame to drop off my application, but thanks to an inattentive security guard and a Sharpie, I do now.

5. **Many eligible players wait for years before being inducted, while others are inducted in their first year of eligibility. Do you have any concerns about timing that we should be aware of?**

❏ Am really hoping to be inducted now before Chris Osgood gets in and ruins it for everybody.

❏ Would rather not be inducted the same year as Eric Lindros, since I don't want my speech to be interrupted by Flyers fans pelting my family with garbage.

❏ Don't want to wait until next year, because I played for a team based in the southern United States, and it would be cool to be inducted while they still exist.

❏ Am worried that Jeremy Roenick may be voted in at some point in the next few years, and don't really feel like sitting through a six-hour induction speech.

6. **Finally, did you ever commit any of the following unpardonable sins (listed in increasing order of severity), which could permanently disqualify you from consideration?**

❏ Committed an act of on-ice violence for which I received a lengthy suspension.

❏ Was involved in an off-ice scandal that damaged my reputation and tarnished my legacy.

❏ Was convicted of unspeakable crimes for which I was sentenced to lengthy jail time.

❏ Once made the media wait a few extra minutes for a post-game interview.

Thank you for applying. Please note that only successful candidates will be contacted.

41

RATING THE NHL'S RELOCATION CANDIDATES

In 2011, the NHL saw a team move for the first time in years, when the Atlanta Thrashers headed to Winnipeg to become the reborn Jets. The destination wasn't a surprise—Winnipeg had been rumored to be in the running for a team for years. But many were expecting that it would be the struggling Phoenix franchise that would be on the move. Instead, the Coyotes stuck around for another year of speculation about an eventual move of their own.

But where? Several cities have been linked with the league in recent years, many with strong cases. But each candidate also comes with a unique set of challenges, and success is far from guaranteed. It goes without saying that the league is under heavy pressure to make the right choice.

I want to help. So I've put together a list of some of the six most frequently mentioned candidates for NHL relocation, and carefully considered the pros and cons of each one.

Hamilton, Ontario

Background: Jim Balsillie has been trying to move a team to the city for years, but has been rejected as a potential NHL owner on the grounds that he has actual money.

Pro: Hockey players are often said to have their best years in their late twenties; if the same applies to hockey arenas, Hamilton should be all set.

Con: If Hamilton ever gets an NHL team then Toronto will want one too, according to the guy in the next cubicle who also still says, "Whazzup?" and quotes dialogue from the Austin Powers movies.

Seattle, Washington

Background: Was actually the first American city to win the Stanley Cup back in 1917, thanks to a late goal by grizzled veteran Mark Recchi.

Pro: Recently had its NBA team blatantly stolen, so probably wouldn't feel too bad about doing the same to some other city.

Con: Vancouver Canucks fans report that unpredictable weather patterns in the Pacific Northwest can sometimes cause springtime heat waves so sudden that fans need to remove their shirts on live television.

Las Vegas, Nevada

Background: Hockey in the desert? That's practically guaranteed to work!

Pro: If the league insists on losing money on a doomed and reckless gamble, it should at least do it somewhere where it'll have company.

Con: Might be hard for fans in attendance to follow the puck, thanks to all the steam rising up from where the ice used to be.

Kansas City, Missouri

Background: Has already tried to lure the Penguins and Islanders in recent years, although that just turned out to be part of a weird plot to try to impress Bryan Trottier.

Pro: Would immediately have a natural geographic rivalry with the St. Louis Blues, and it would be a nice change for someone in the hockey world to remember that the Blues still exist.

Con: The city is called Kansas City but is not located in Kansas, which probably doesn't impact its ability to support a hockey team, but has always just kind of bothered me.

Markham, Ontario

Background: This town north of Toronto is working towards building an NHL-ready arena, after residents complained that the traffic jams on the 404 weren't quite long enough.

Pro: Falls just outside of Buffalo's boundary for compensation, and screwing over the Sabres on a technicality is one of hockey's richest traditions.

Con: Might not be the first choice of the NHL, which tends to prefer that teams are located in large cities, or medium-sized cities, or small cities, or any kind of actual city.

Quebec City, Quebec

Background: The Nordiques made the mistake of trading for Wendel Clark in 1994; being forced to leave Toronto made him so sad he punched the entire franchise to Colorado.

Pro: Could immediately resume a rivalry with the Montreal Canadiens, which would be great because that worked out so well for Quebec City the last time around.

Con: The city's population must not be very interested in hockey anymore, because if you go around town asking, "Who is your favorite NHL player?" most people just stare at you like you're speaking a different language.

WHAT AN OFFICIAL NHL SUSPENSION CALL REALLY SOUNDS LIKE

Hockey fans have become very familiar with suspensions over the past few years. Whether it was Colin Campbell or Brendan Shanahan handing out the justice, it seems like there's a new decision being announced every few days. So by now, fans know the drill. A serious infraction results in the perpetrator receiving an invitation to an in-person hearing at the league office, while lesser offenses are handled over the phone.

But what does that phone call sound like? Most fans probably imagine a lengthy conference call in which agents, player reps, and league officials all get a chance to weigh in before a final verdict is reached.

As it turns out, it's not that complicated. DGB spies got hold of the hotline number, and here's a transcript of what they heard.

Thank you for calling the National Hockey League's suspension hotline. For service in English, press one. *Pour le service en Français, appuyer sur le deux.* For service in Randy Cunneyworth's version of French, pressez-vous à the numero three now.

You have selected English. Please note that your call may be monitored for training purposes, since we're all assuming Shanahan will wise up and tell Bettman to stuff this job within a year.

Please indicate what you did wrong to deserve this phone hearing:

If you slashed somebody, press one.

If you hit somebody from behind, press two.

If you took out somebody's knees, press three.

If took out somebody's knees by slashing them from behind, press four.

If you hit somebody in the head, press five.

If you have no idea what you did because you're a Boston Bruin and the local media keeps insisting you did nothing wrong, please stay on the line and one of our operators will be pleased to assist you.

You have pressed five, for a head shot.

You will now have an opportunity to defend yourself for hitting another player in the head. Please enter the excuse you would like us to politely listen to and then ignore:

If you're claiming that you didn't actually make contact with the other guy's head and are really hoping nobody in this office has access to YouTube, press one.

If you didn't mean to hurt anybody, and were just trying to get yourself suspended so that you wouldn't have to attend the All-Star Game, press two.

If you used to room with Brendan Shanahan back in his playing days and assume he doesn't want anyone to see those photos you still have, press three.

If you don't see what the big deal is about flagrant head shots, dial four on the rotary phone you're presumably using, since you are trapped in 1950.

If you can't think of an excuse because you haven't had a chance to talk to your team's PR person yet, press five.

You have pressed 5. We will now determine the length of your suspension.

Please enter your salary and the line that you play on, followed by the pound sign.

Please enter the salary of the guy you laid out and the line he plays on, followed by the pound sign.

You have indicated that you are a fourth liner, and the guy you laid out was a superstar. Would you like to just retire now and save everyone some time? Press one for yes and two for no.

You have pressed two for no. Thanks for nothing, Raffi.

Finally, when Brendan Shanahan announces your suspension he will release a video explaining his decision on Twitter and NHL.com. Please describe how you would like him to appear during his video:

If you would like him to awkwardly stare into the camera while looking tired, press one.

If you would like him to awkwardly stare into the camera while looking annoyed, press two.

If you would like him to awkwardly stare into the camera while looking exasperated, press three.

If you would like him to awkwardly stare into the camera while looking like he cannot believe he has to explain this rule to you idiots all over again, press four.

If you would like him to do all of the above at the same time while being shot from the waist up in a way that makes it disturbingly unclear whether or not he is wearing pants, press five.

You have pressed five for all of the above.

This completes your phone hearing. You will be notified of Brendan Shanahan's decision later today. In the meantime, please answer one additional question.

Has the league's discipline process given you a better appreciation of the importance of player safety, which will deter you from this sort of dangerous behavior in the future? Press one for yes or two for no.

You have delivered a leaping elbow smash to two for no. Sigh. We figured as much. (*Click*)

OTHER MARIO LEMIEUX GRIEVANCES

One thing you can say about Mario Lemieux: When he gets cranky, he's not too concerned about who knows it.

For example, we all remember the 2011 game between the Islanders and Penguins that turned into a gong show, featuring several line brawls and accusations of goon tactics on the part of New York. Lemieux decided to share some feedback, releasing a statement ripping into the league and its leadership, calling the events "unacceptable and embarrassing" and hinting that he could leave the sport entirely if things didn't improve.

Many applauded his stance, while others were critical or even accused him of hypocrisy. But those critics may want to brace themselves, because sources in Pittsburgh tell me that the Islanders game was just one of a long list of things that are severely ticking Mario off:

- Today's players don't seem to grasp the fundamentals, with many unable to execute even a basic "intentionally lose the puck in the defenseman's skates to distract him long enough to blow by him and score" move.

- He hasn't played a league game for over five years now, so he's not really sure why Esa Tikkanen is still following him around and yapping in his ear all day.

- While all the cheap shots and fighting during that Islanders game were hard to take, New York really went over the line with that lengthy pre-game ceremony retiring David Volek's number.

- While occasional encounters with die-hard Penguins fans are nice, the endless gushing, autograph demands, and girlish squeals of admiration make it sort of tough to get anything done during meetings with Gary Bettman.

- All these gosh darn Stanley Cup rings make it really tough to raise a hand to give Garth Snow the finger.

- Hey, you try writing a thoughtful statement about the current state of the game with Matt Cooke elbowing you in the head the entire time.

- The revelation that Zenon Konopka once had a poster of him in his bedroom really makes Mario question whether everything he accomplished in his career was really worth it.

- You have one little physical confrontation with referee Kerry Fraser early in your career, and you can never go out in public again without every Leaf fan you see trying to hug you.

- While he realizes that the NHL Guardian Project superheroes were meant to honor key aspects of a franchise's history, he's still not crazy about the Penguin's superpower being "mulletude."

- Whenever all the owners get together for a scrimmage, Ted Leonsis won't stop asking him if he wants some advice on improving his game.

- Ever since Sidney Crosby moved out, Saturday morning "chocolate-chip pancakes and cartoons in pajamas" time just isn't the same.

- Those 1987 Canada Cup team reunions just get awkward when everyone has to pretend to know who Doug Crossman is.

- As a forty-six-year-old with bad hips and a history of back problems, must somehow come to grips with the fact that he could probably only score 120 or 130 points if he was still playing today.

- Despite all of his frequent and passionate requests, it turns out that if you actually sneak up behind Mike Lange after a goal and scratch his back with a hacksaw he'll scream like a child and call the police.

UNDERSTANDING THE NEW WAVE OF ADVANCED STATISTICS

While anyone can recite traditional stats like goals, assists, and plus/minus, these days many fans are turning to more advanced statistics that can help shed even more light on player performance. Some of these stats are even starting to turn up in mainstream media reports or broadcasts, and there are rumors that some front offices may be using them to help with roster decisions.

Unfortunately, while advanced stat proponents do an excellent job of using data to analyze the action on the ice, they're often not quite so good at explaining things in layman's terms. It's fairly common to see a reference to an advanced stat with no explanation of what it means or why it's important, which can be frustrating to a casual fan.

So while I can't exactly claim to be an expert, I want to help. I want to help so badly that I was willing to spend a few seconds googling terms in an attempt to figure out what they mean. So if you'd like to get on board the advanced stats bandwagon, here are ten of the most important terms you may encounter:

QualComp: This stat, short for "Quality of Competition," measures the strength of the opposition a player typically faces. A player with a very high QualComp probably plays against the other team's top lines. A player with a low Qual-Comp score probably plays against below-average competition. A player with an extremely low QualComp score probably plays in the Northwest Division and gets to face Edmonton and Calgary a lot.

Corsi: Corsi is similar to the traditional plus/minus stat, except that it counts all shots directed at the net rather than just goals. This results in a more reliable measure due to larger sample size, because the number of shots taken will always be higher than the number of goals scored. Unless the opposition is starting Steve Mason in net, in which case the numbers will be equal.

Relative Corsi: This stat is a player's Corsi number when he's on the ice with his twin brother.

Fenwick: Essentially the same as Corsi, except it excludes blocked shots from the calculation. If you are caught wearing Corsi colors in a Fenwick neighborhood, you will be stabbed.

Zone Starts: You can learn a lot about players based on which zone they typically start in. For example, a player who starts most of his game in the Eastern time zone plays for a team that is important and will be on television a lot, while a player who starts most of his games in a Western time zone can safely be ignored.

TOI/60: This is an abbreviation for "time on ice per 60 minutes," and measures how much ice time a player receives over the course of an average game. You can learn a lot about a team from checking this stat. For example, if a team has five players who all have a 60.0 in this category, it means the team has forgotten to go into the game settings menu and turn line changes on.

ESSV%: This stands for "even strength save percentage" and measures a goalie's ability to stop the puck when teams are playing five-on-five, with .920 being average and anything over .930 being excellent. It is not to be confused with ENSV% or "empty net save percentage," which measures a goalie's ability to stop the puck when his team has pulled him for an extra attacker, with .000 being average and anything over .000 being excellent and, come to think of it, we probably don't really need this stat.

Regression to the mean: This mathematical concept means that anything going well in your life will inevitably start getting worse again and make you sad. Statisticians are incredibly depressing to hang out with.

PDO: This stat adds up a team's shooting percentage and save percentage while a specific player is on the ice. Since this tends to regress to 1000 over a large enough sample size, it can be used to measure whether or not a player is benefitting from unsustainably good luck. Used in a sentence: "On the day he was introduced to Carrie Underwood, Mike Fisher's PDO was off the charts."

Wins: This stat measures the number of times a goaltender has been credited with a win. It's extremely useful for determining if the person you are talking to is a fan of advanced statistical analysis, since casually mentioning goaltender wins during the course of a conversation will immediately cause a blood vessel in their forehead to explode.

45

A BRIEF HISTORY OF
TEEMU SELANNE

One of the best moments of the 2011–12 season came in mid-December when Anaheim's Teemu Selanne made his long-awaited return to Winnipeg. It had been over fifteen years since Selanne had played a game in the city, but fans there hadn't forgotten the magic moments he created as a Jet in the early nineties. Once the NHL announced the return of a franchise to Winnipeg, fans circled that night's game on their calendars.

The emotional ovation was just the latest in a long list of highlights for one of the game's classiest and most popular superstars. Let's take a look back at Selanne's memorable career:

June 11, 1988: Selanne is drafted with the tenth overall pick by Winnipeg Jets general manager John Ferguson Sr., who must then explain to his confused son why he's not immediately trading him for a terrible backup goalie.

October 8, 1992: Veteran Jets defenseman Randy Carlyle refuses Selanne's request for his jersey number—#8— then wonders why the rookie is walking away mumbling something about "payback" and "revenge" and "Bruce Boudreau in twenty years."

March 2, 1993: Selanne breaks Mike Bossy's rookie goal-scoring record and then famously mimes shooting his glove out of the air, while a young Artem Anisimov watches at home imagining how everyone would probably think it was really cool if he did something like that someday.

June 17, 1993: After finishing the season with 76 goals and 132 points, Selanne wins the Calder Trophy for top rookie in a close vote over the two other finalists, "Ha ha ha" and "No seriously, Teemu Selanne had 76 goals and 132 points this year, why are we even voting on this?"

April 4, 1995: My wife finally realizes that the flashy kid on the Jets who scores all those goals is not in fact named "T. Mussolini" in a moment that I wish I was making up.

February 7, 1996: Selanne is traded to the Anaheim Mighty Ducks, which devastated Winnipeg Jets fans assume will be the worst thing to happen to them all year.

January 18, 1998: Selanne scores a hat trick and is named MVP of the All-Star Game, putting to rest the old stereo-type that Europeans just don't want to win badly enough when it comes to intolerably dull corporate shill-fests.

March 5, 2001: The Mighty Ducks trade Selanne to San Jose Sharks, but hold open the possibility that he could always return to the franchise in four or five years as a con-sultant or an assistant scout or a dominant first-line winger.

July 3, 2003: Selanne signs a heavily discounted free agent deal to join the Colorado Avalanche for one season that nobody remembers because it *never happened*.

September 15, 2004: A slumping and aging Selanne returns to his native Finland to undergo knee surgery during the NHL lockout, since having all your internal organs replaced with titanium cyborg parts is apparently called "knee surgery" in Finland.

June 6, 2007: Even during his most triumphant moment, the classy Selanne insists on sharing the credit with those who made it all possible, which makes it kind of awkward when he goes to hand the Stanley Cup to Chris Phillips.

January 28, 2008: Selanne announces that he will return to the Ducks for one final season, on the condition that everyone agrees to act surprised when he makes the exact same announcement every off-season for the rest of his life.

February 20, 2010: An assist in Finland's win over Germany makes Selanne the all-time scoring leader in Olympic hockey, although the record is broken a few days later by every single Canadian player who gets a shift against Evgeni Nabokov.

March 28, 2011: Selanne becomes the oldest player in NHL history to score on a penalty shot, then regales his younger teammates with stories of days long ago when penalty shots were still considered exciting, back before Gary Bettman brought in the shoot-out and ruined them.

December 17, 2011: As the heartfelt pre-game ovation from Winnipeg fans grows louder by the moment, with no signs of letting up, Teemu Selanne begins to get the feeling that he may have been in this city before and should possibly remember who any of these people are.

OTHER WAYS NHL TEAMS USE HOME ICE ADVANTAGE FOR AN UNFAIR EDGE

When the talk of the entire hockey world is a mid-season game between the Kings and Blue Jackets, you have to assume that something has gone horribly wrong. And midway through the 2011 season, you'd have been right.

A game in Los Angeles between the two teams was decided on a late Drew Doughty goal that seemed to cross the goal line with a fraction of a second left on the clock. But replays showed something mysterious: The game clock appeared to pause for over one full second right before the goal. That slight delay was enough to turn a goal that shouldn't have counted into the game winner.

Predictably, conspiracy theories were floated immediately. The league promised a thorough investigation, while making clear that the game's results would stand. Everyone was outraged.

Should they have been? No. Because even if the glitch was intentional, it wouldn't be unique. After all, the Kings wouldn't be the first hockey team to get a little boost from their home arena. In fact, it's common practice. Here are just a few of the ways that teams around the league are using their rinks to gain unfair advantage:

New York Islanders: Attempt to unnerve opposing players by ensuring that the visiting team's dressing room is infested with vicious disease-carrying rats that are slightly larger than the rats infesting the home team's room.

Toronto Maple Leafs: Thanks to the typical midweek crowds at the ACC, are often able to get out to a quick start against confused opponents, who can take up to two full periods to realize that the pre-game moment of silence has ended.

Tampa Bay Lightning: Blatantly attempt to damage the retinas of opposing players by placing a bright red light directly behind their own goaltender and turning it on three or four times every period.

Vancouver Canucks: An intricate installation of mirrors and holographic lasers has actually succeeded in convincing foolish opponents that the Canucks' best player has a linemate who looks exactly like him.

Minnesota Wild: While visiting teams have made clear that they realize every arena has imperfections and they don't want to seem like they're whining, they'd still prefer an indoor dressing room.

Montreal Canadiens: Have been known to attempt to confuse opponents by having their fans loudly engage in chants from the wrong sport.

Detroit Red Wings: Players visiting Joe Louis Arena often report feeling confused and disoriented by the experience of playing in an arena that doesn't have some faceless corporation's name slapped all over it.

Winnipeg Jets: After years of playing fair in Atlanta, have achieved an unfair advantage recently by filling their building with fans who actually care about hockey.

New Jersey Devils: While they concede that it doesn't actually create a competitive advantage, visiting teams report that it's still kind of weird how all the benches and penalty boxes in the arena suddenly have little tip jars.

Pittsburgh Penguins: Oh sure, *you* try to concentrate knowing Jean-Claude Van Damme might be battling terrorists on the catwalk overhead.

Edmonton Oilers: At one point last year, instructed the official scorekeeper to start randomly assigning a point to Sam Gagner on every single goal scored, just to see if anyone noticed.

Boston Bruins: Opponents report that due to an apparent architectural error, the path to the Bruins net is constantly blocked by some sort of huge granite pillar wearing a #33 jersey.

Ottawa Senators: After an afternoon of leisurely pre-game preparation, it's always fun for the Senator players to see their opponents sprinting off their team bus three minutes before puck drop while breathlessly screaming, "Seriously, that's the closest spot to downtown you could find to build your arena?"

SEVENTH HEAVEN

When One Game Decides the Stanley Cup

Game seven. Those two words are all but guaranteed to get a hockey fan's blood boiling. There's something almost poetic about a hard-fought series ending with one winner-takes-all game. And when that game seven comes in the Stanley Cup final, the drama can be almost unbearable. With the Cup in the building and up for grabs, every play is crucial and every player knows he has a chance to create his legacy.

For a long time, a game seven in the final was one of the rarest sights in hockey. The best-of-seven format was adopted in 1939, but only eight series went the distance over the next forty-eight years. More recently, though, fans have been spoiled. If you only started watching hockey in 1987, you've been lucky enough to see a seventh and deciding game in the Stanley Cup final eight different times.

Let's take a look back at the past twenty-five years' worth of game-seven drama.

1987: Edmonton Oilers 3, Philadelphia Flyers 1

The memorable moment: Glenn Anderson scores the insurance goal on a long slap shot, proving the old hockey adage that you can't win the Cup without contributions from your sixth or seventh best future hall-of-famer.

The hero: Losing goaltender Ron Hextall was the obvious choice in voting for the Conn Smythe Trophy as play-off MVP, according to a dazed NHL official crumpled on the floor with a broken goal stick near his head.

The legacy: After losing the Stanley Cup final despite an excellent goaltending performance, the Flyers' front office vows never to make that mistake again.

1994: New York Rangers 3, Vancouver Canucks 2

The memorable moment: A generation of Canuck fans learn that LaFayette is a French name deriving from *la* meaning "the," and *fayette* meaning "puck just hit the post oh my lord what did we ever do to make the hockey gods hate us so much?"

The hero: Mark Messier scored the winning goal, creating the last known instance in his career of him having an impact in a game involving the Vancouver Canucks.

The legacy: The game would go down in history as one of the most watched in NHL history with over five million viewers, and that's just from the one hundred people at a time who tune in whenever it gets replayed on the *NHL Network*.

2001: Colorado Avalanche 3, New Jersey Devils 1

The memorable moment: Fans around the world tuned into the game to see legendary defenseman Ray Bourque win his first Stanley Cup, since they figured that even if the Devils were winning he'd just request a trade to them instead.

The hero: Alex Tanguay records three points and later credits injured teammate Peter Forsberg for inspiring him, although he'll admit that next time he could probably do with a simple motivational speech instead of that whole "leave your ruptured spleen on the top shelf of my locker" thing.

The legacy: This would be the final Stanley Cup win of Patrick Roy's career. Since Roy had previously claimed to have the first few championship rings in his ears, Jeremy Roenick was happy to suggest an alternate location where he could stick this one.

2003: New Jersey Devils 3, Anaheim Mighty Ducks 0

The memorable moment: Paul Kariya's shocking return to the ice after a devastating hit from Scott Stevens was so dramatic and memorable that hockey fans around the world agreed to forget it actually happened in game six instead of in this excruciatingly boring game.

The hero: Despite the Ducks losing the series, the Conn Smythe was unanimously awarded to the larger-than-life star of the playoffs that loomed over everything, Jean-Sebastien Giguere's shoulder pads.

The legacy: While he admired their skill and didn't doubt that they could be back in the final someday, Scott Niedermayer couldn't help but wonder why all the Anaheim players in the handshake line kept pressing dollar bills into his palm and winking at him.

2004: Tampa Bay Lightning 2, Calgary Flames 1

The memorable moment: As jubilant Tampa Bay players vow to be right back in the final next year, Gary Bettman is heard mumbling, "You mean in 2005? Yeah, don't get your hopes up."

The hero: Ruslan Fedotenko's second goal gives the Lightning their fourth game-winning goal of the Stanley Cup final, tying a record set most recently by the Flames in game six.

The legacy: Disappointed Flames fans console themselves that at least they got to game seven of the final, which is further than those losers in Edmonton will ever get.

2006: Carolina Hurricanes 3, Edmonton Oilers 1

The hero: Cam Ward is the first rookie in twenty years to win the Conn Smythe and instantly becomes the most recognizable hockey player in Carolina history, according to one guy who kind of squints at him the next day before shrugging and walking away.

The memorable moment: Gary Bettman's press conference extolling the virtues of the new salary cap and its benefits for small-market teams is cut short when he's chased out of the building by torch- and pitchfork-wielding TV executives.

The legacy: Despite many so-called experts trying to write off their playoff run as a fluke, Chris Pronger assures Oilers fans that he has every intention of being right back in the final next year.

2009: Pittsburgh Penguins 2, Detroit Red Wings 1

The memorable moment: The Penguins finally clinch their first championship of the Sidney Crosby era, when Nicklas Lidstrom's last-second scoring chance is thwarted on a spectacular diving goalmouth save by Gary Bettman.

The hero: Unheralded grinder Maxime Talbot comes out of nowhere to score both Pittsburgh goals, leading fans around the world to remark that they'd never noticed how much he looks like Penguins owner Mario Lemieux wearing a fake moustache and glasses.

The legacy: Everyone agrees that the Penguins are going to win a ton of Stanley Cups as long as this Sidney Crosby kid stays healthy.

2011: Boston Bruins 4, Vancouver Canucks 0

The memorable moment: With the Vancouver net vacant in favor of an extra attacker, Brad Marchand clinches the win with an empty-net goal, which Canucks fans unanimously agree Roberto Luongo should have had.

The hero: Bruins coaches inspire Tim Thomas to a spectacular shutout performance by filling the net behind him with baby bald eagles swaddled in the original copy of the Constitution of the United States.

The legacy: Hockey fans everywhere are reminded once again of three age-old truths: Goaltending wins championships, team toughness is crucial in the playoffs, and it's a really bad idea to tag yourself in riot photos on Facebook.

HOW TO DOMINATE YOUR FANTASY HOCKEY LEAGUE

The hockey pool is an annual tradition for many fans. Training camp is winding down, the season is just around the corner, and all around North America friends and colleagues gather in boardrooms and bars to draft the fantasy teams that will lead them on a path to glory.

Well, maybe not so much glory. For most fans, it's more like a path to frustration, second-guessing, and regret. After all, only one team can take home the league title in any given year. Everyone else will be left to look back on the draft day mistakes that cost them the championship.

It doesn't have to be that way. With a little bit of focus and a clear strategy, you too can dominate your hockey pool. All you need to do is follow these simple tips:

- Be aware of your league's roster rules and the potential consequences of not following them. For example, failing to have two NHL goaltenders on your roster can result in invalid lineups, forfeited matchups, and a front office job offer from the Flyers.

- Despite still indicating his interest in a comeback, Vesa Toskala has yet to sign with an NHL team. Until he does, don't forget to reduce your scoring projections for every player in the league by about 25 percent.

- Every year there are a few players who greatly exceed even the most optimistic projections, and who can almost single-handedly determine the winner of a pool. You should probably try to figure out who those guys are going to be this year and then draft a whole bunch of them.

- When it's time to collect everyone's twenty bucks for the prize pool, ask Sabres owner Terry Pegula if he'd be willing to kick in an extra $10 million up front for no reason. He usually agrees to that.

- For extra NHL authenticity, remind everyone in the first round of your draft to waste everybody's time with long-winded congratulations to last year's champion and their thanks to whoever is hosting this year's event.

- Just for fun, take Paul Bissonnette in the last round then send him a message about it on Twitter. He'll probably find that every bit as hilarious as he did the first 500 times it happened.

- As much fun as a fantasy league can be, never lose sight of the fact that the players you're drafting are more than just names in a row on a spreadsheet. They're also characters from your favorite hockey video game.

- A "sleeper" is a player capable of putting up big numbers, but who remains unknown to most fans. To find one, try building a time machine and traveling back to before we had the Internet.

- Jarome Iginla should be at the center of any decent draft strategy. Actually, that's not true—I just wanted to be the first hockey writer to ever use "Jarome Iginla" and "decent" and "center" in the same sentence.

- Many experts will tell you to avoid Russian players, since as Europeans they're lazy and selfish and refuse to work as hard as North Americans do. This is utter nonsense; Russia is technically part of Asia.

- Playoff pools: When faced with a choice between two players with similar talent levels and statistical output, it's generally a good idea to lean towards the one whose team qualified for the post-season.

- Sure, it's always more fun to play in a pool with an "easy money" guy who puts together a terrible team that finishes dead last every year. But Scott Howson already told you that he's busy this week, so stop calling him.

- Don't be that guy who goes to a hockey game and yells at the players to let them know they're on your fantasy team. To really get their attention, whisper it from under their beds just as they're falling asleep.

49

A PERIOD-BY-PERIOD RECAP OF THE 2012 STANLEY CUP FINAL

The 2012 Stanley Cup final matchup was, on the surface, a tough one to get excited about. The Kings and Devils had no real history together, there was essentially zero rivalry in place before the series started, and there were few if any ready-made storylines to focus on. Many expected that the series could wind up being a forgettable dud, and they looked like they'd be right when the Kings shot out to a 3–0 lead.

And then, almost without warning, the series took a turn. The Devils mounted an admirable comeback, extending the series twice before finally falling in an entertaining sixth game. So while the series isn't likely to be remembered as an all-time classic, it did end up providing its share of memorable moments.

Let's take a period-by-period look back at the 2012 Stanley Cup final:

Game One: Kings 2, Devils 1 (OT)

First period: The opening face-off is delayed briefly when NHL officials have to spend time reminding the Kings that "hockey" is a fun sport that they all used to enjoy playing right until their third-round series ended six weeks ago.

Second period: Anton Volchenkov scores for the Devils, delighting all those fans who drafted him as a sleeper in the 4,000th round of their playoff pool.

Third period: It's possible that all the neutral zone trapping, clutch-and-grab defensive play, and constant shot-blocking might be making these games a little less entertaining than they could be, Martin Brodeur and Jonathan Quick agree during an extended conversation at center ice as the period goes on.

Overtime: The Kings win the game by catching New Jersey off guard by executing a rarely seen play they refer to as "pass the puck directly to our best player who is skating down the middle of the ice with nobody covering him for some reason."

Game Two: Kings 2, Devils 1 (OT)

First period: To mark the first game of the season to be played in June, the NHL apparently decides to air a summer re-run.

Second period: Fun trivia: According to the detailed research of league historians, this period did in fact exist despite nobody on the planet having a single memory of it.

Third period: While it's understandable that nobody wants a repeat of Marty McSorley's infamous illegal curve penalty from late in game two of the 1993 final, it still seems kind of excessive when the Kings play the entire third period using ringette sticks.

Overtime: Jeff Carter looked pretty good during the replay of his winning goal right up until that sledgehammer smashed through the screen, report people watching the game at Jack Johnson's house.

Game Three: Kings 4, Devils 0

First period: The Kings decide that it's time for Simon Gagne to make his return to the lineup, after they hear a rumor that there's still one Philadelphia Flyer fan left on the planet who doesn't hate them.

Second period: Somewhere, deep in the bowels of the arena, 2012 Dean Lombardi steps into the time machine to travel back and convince 2010 Dean Lombardi to back off on the bidding and just let Ilya Kovalchuk sign with the Devils.

Third period: The Devils' coaching staff begins to toy with the idea of making a radical change to their power play, such as maybe putting an extra guy out there sometimes.

Game Four: Devils 3, Kings 1

First period: Roughly 90 percent of the celebrities who will later claim to be diehard Kings fans become aware of the fact that this series is being played.

Second period: After the Stanley Cup's handlers explain that the case they're carrying holds something that's world famous, 120 years old, and takes twenty people to lift it, excited LA arena workers exclaim that they've always wanted to meet Jack Nicholson.

Third period: In one of those hilarious practical jokes that veterans are always playing on gullible rookies, the Devils wait until there are a few minutes left in the third period of a tie game and then convince Adam Henrique that overtime has already started.

Game Five: Devils 2, Kings 1

First period: Zach Parise realizes you have a chance to score on Jonathan Quick if you can execute a quick one-timer off a cross-ice pass, assuming the pass comes from thirty feet away and is made by Jonathan Quick.

Second period: An apparent goal by Jarret Stoll is waved off due to a high-stick, which is unfortunate because it took him a long time to climb all the way to the top of the arena rafters first.

Third period: Alexei Ponikarovsky and Dustin Penner are given roughing penalties after a late-game scrum that starts over an argument about whether it's a more amazing feeling to be traded away from the Maple Leafs or the Oilers.

Game Six: Kings 6, Devils 1

First period: With one ill-advised boarding major, Steve Bernier instantly becomes the single worst thing to happen to people living in New Jersey since living in New Jersey.

Second period: The Devils' attempt at a comeback is frustrated when every shot they try to take is immediately blocked by a member of the media who doesn't want to fly back to Newark.

Third period: As the seconds tick down and the Kings pile onto the ice to celebrate the franchise's first Stanley Cup win, somewhere, Bill Buckner knowingly clinks glasses with Marty McSorley.

50

NHL HOCKEY,
THEN VS. NOW

There's a romantic view of hockey as some sort of permanent, stable presence in the sporting world. And there's some truth to that. At its heart, the game that today's children lace up and play in rinks and on ponds around the world is similar to the one that past generations enjoyed.

But it's also true that modern hockey fans have seen the sport go through a seemingly endless series of changes in recent years. We've had expansion, work stoppages, new technology, improved equipment, and a constant influx of new rules that can make it hard to keep up with what's happening on and off the ice. In some sense, the current version of the sport is almost unrecognizable when compared to how the league looked just a half-century ago.

Just how different is today's NHL from the one our parents and grandparents enjoyed? Here are some of the key differences that have resulted from the league's continuing evolution:

Then: Players wore flimsy pads on their shoulders and elbows that didn't provide much protection, so the risk of injury was high.

Now: The game is much safer thanks to the advent of modern protective padding, like the Carbonite Skull-Crusher 3000.

Now: Players demonstrate their commitment to fitness by adhering to a strict diet, carefully monitoring their body fat index, and maintaining a rigorous year-round training program.

Then: Players demonstrated their commitment to fitness by trying really hard to smoke only between shifts.

Then: During breaks between play, fans filled in the quiet moments by having conversations with fellow fans about the game they were watching.

Now: During breaks between play, fans fill in the quiet moments by blinking once before the arena host starts screeching trivia questions and sponsor messages at them.

Now: On the way home from the game, fans can complain about the team's superstar to their cabdriver, who will likely agree that the player is wildly overpaid.

Then: On the way home from the game, fans could start to complain about the team's superstar to their cabdriver, before realizing it was him.

Then: There were only six teams in the league, meaning that when American TV networks planned their broadcast schedule, they had only six teams to choose from.

Now: There are thirty teams in the league, meaning that when American TV networks plan their broadcast schedule, they have only six teams to choose from.

Now: Players occasionally engage in "staged fights," which all reasonable fans and media agree are an embarrassment to hockey's rich history of sportsmanship.

Then: Players never engaged in "staged fights," preferring to settle disputes with more gentlemanly methods such as spontaneously hitting each other over the head with their sticks before climbing into the stands to attack some fans.

Then: As hard as it is for today's fans to imagine, goaltenders used to play without wearing masks.

Now: Goaltenders have long since realized that masks are absolutely essential, since otherwise there'd be nowhere for them to paint pictures of their favorite celebrities and cartoon characters.

Now: Players who suffer a head injury and are unable to immediately return to the game are sent to the "quiet room," which is a term for a medical examination room in the arena where they can be evaluated in more detail.

Then: Players who suffered a head injury and were unable to immediately return to the game were sent to the "quiet room," a term for the unemployment office.

Then: Fans watching on black-and-white television sets wished that the games could be broadcast in color.

Now: Fans watching on high-definition television sets wish that the games could be broadcast in black and white, at least whenever Don Cherry's latest suit appears on the screen.

Now: Fans sometimes get to see games decided by an exciting event known as the shoot-out.

Then: Fans were forced to suffer through the monotony of seeing the game's results determined entirely by actual hockey.

Then: The widespread use of curved stick blades increased offense, because they made slap shots behave unpredictably.

Now: Modern composite sticks increase offense, because they disintegrate in a defenseman's hand any time there's a slight breeze in the arena.

Now: If you leap to your feet and mercilessly boo Gary Bettman as soon as he makes an appearance at the game, you can count on your fellow fans joining in.

Then: If you leapt to your feet and mercilessly booed Gary Bettman as soon as he made an appearance at the game, you could count on your fellow fans turning to you and asking if that didn't seem kind of harsh for Little League.

Then: The All-Star Game featured a collection of the league's best players competing against the reigning Stanley Cup champions.

Now: The All-Star Game is totally different, in the sense that it no longer features anybody competing against anyone.

Now: A player who notices two referees arguing with each other would suspect that an especially close play has just occurred and the officials are taking the time to make sure they get the call right.

Then: A player who noticed two referees arguing with each other would suspect that he was still a little hungover from the night before.

Then: The one thing hockey fans could count on was seeing the Stanley Cup awarded every year, unless there was a major tragedy, such as a deadly outbreak of influenza.

Now: The one thing hockey fans can count on is seeing the Stanley Cup awarded every year, unless there's a major tragedy, such as a disagreement over how best to link player salaries to league revenues.

AN IN-DEPTH COMPARISON

Eric Lindros vs. Peter Forsberg

It's hard to think of two recent NHL superstars whose careers were more intertwined than Eric Lindros and Peter Forsberg. Both were chosen early in the 1991 draft, both won the Hart Trophy, both were considered the best player in hockey at some point, and both were plagued by multiple injuries that forced them to miss extensive time and ultimately cut their careers short.

The most famous connection, of course, is even more direct: the controversial 1992 trade that saw Lindros dealt from Quebec to Philadelphia in exchange for a package that included Forsberg, multiple players and draft picks, and $15 million in cash. In addition to being one of the most significant trades in NHL history, the deal all but guaranteed that the two players would be compared to each other throughout their careers.

But how similar were they? Let's take a closer look at the careers of these two hockey legends:

Peter Forsberg: Was known as "Peter the Great" for most of his NHL career, although fans back in Sweden were more likely to refer to him as *Foppa*.

Eric Lindros: Was known as "The Big E" for most of his NHL career, although fans back in Quebec City were more likely to refer to him as something we can't print in this book due to obscenity laws.

Eric Lindros: Won the Hart Trophy as MVP in 1995 but never won it a second time, disappointing notoriously tough Philadelphia Flyers fans.

Peter Forsberg: Won the Calder Trophy as rookie of the year in 1995 but never won it a second time, disappointing Colorado Avalanche fans who didn't quite have the hang of this whole thing yet.

Peter Forsberg: Is the son of Kent Forsberg, who coached the Swedish national team from 1995 to 1998.

Eric Lindros: Is the son of Bonnie and Carl Lindros, who coached every team Eric ever played on, they thought.

Eric Lindros: Combined with John LeClair and Mikael Renberg to form a line that became known as The Legion of Doom because they were physically imposing and offensively dominant.

Peter Forsberg: Combined with Milan Hejduk and Alex Tanguay to form a line that became known as The AMP Line because of the NHL's strictly enforced "only one line per decade gets an actual creative nickname that doesn't involve just taking all their initials and making it spell a word" rule.

Peter Forsberg: Made an international impact at the 1994 Olympics by scoring the gold medal winning shoot-out goal with a one-handed deke, which was later honored on a postage stamp.

Eric Lindros: Made an international impact at the 1991 Canada Cup by breaking Ulf Samuelsson's shoulder with a body check that should have been honored on a postage stamp, according to all these petitions from Cam Neely.

Eric Lindros: His dramatic return to the Flyers lineup during the 2000 playoffs ended after just two games, when he was on the receiving end of a vicious body check from Scott Stevens.

Peter Forsberg: His dramatic return to the Avalanche lineup during the 2011 season ended after just two games, when he was on the receiving end of a vicious reality check from Father Time.

Peter Forsberg: Was unable to participate in the final two playoff rounds in 2001 after suffering a serious injury that resulted in doctors removing his spleen.

Eric Lindros: Was unable to participate in any playoff rounds at all in 2006 after signing a contract to play for the Toronto Maple Leafs.

Eric Lindros: Has been the subject of a bizarre and implausible urban legend involving a bar fight with figure skater Elvis Stojko.

Peter Forsberg: Has been the subject of a bizarre and implausible urban legend involving him once having played for the Nashville Predators.

Peter Forsberg: Achieved his ultimate goal by helping the Avalanche win the Stanley Cup in 1996 and 2001.

Eric Lindros: Never did manage to achieve his ultimate goal, since Bobby Clarke never had his back turned when there was a folding chair nearby.

Eric Lindros: Played against the Red Wings in one playoff series as a member of the Flyers, after which the brooms came out because Detroit won in four straight.

Peter Forsberg: Played against the Red Wings in five different playoff series as a member of the Avalanche, after which the brooms came out because can you think of a better way to clean up all those teeth?

Peter Forsberg: His many injuries included a recurring looseness in his ankle in 2006, which Flyers team doctors described as a "ligament laxity."

Eric Lindros: His many injuries included a collapsed lung in 1999, which Flyers team doctors described as "no big deal, just get on the airplane, you big baby."

Eric Lindros: Announced his retirement at a 2007 press conference, which was briefly interrupted when he was overcome with emotion at the thought of his playing career being over.

Peter Forsberg: Announced his retirement at a 2008 press conference, which was briefly interrupted by his announcement of his comeback, which was briefly interrupted by his announcement of his retirement from that comeback, which was briefly interrupted by all the reporters leaving while he was still talking.

52

TAKE THE QUIZ

Was that a Dive?

While occasional "embellishment" has always been a hockey fact of life, recent years have seen diving elevated to an art form. It now seems like you can't go a week without players, coaches, and media complaining that certain opponents are taking the dramatics too far.

The problem has become so noticeable that last year the NHL reportedly issued a directive to officials to call more diving penalties. But that move just appears to have created more controversy, with some players being whistled for penalties even when they'd been legitimately hauled down.

It's all very frustrating. Short of using lie detector tests or hiring a mind reader, how can a fan really tell whether a player was diving?

Luckily, the league is on the case. Working with officials and forensic experts, they've put together this handy quiz for fans watching the game at home. From now on, if you think you may have witnessed a dive, simply take a few minutes to answer these questions and arrive at a definitive answer:

1. **A player is rolling around on the ice while clutching his head after a borderline penalty. Which of the following would make you suspect a dive?**

   A) The offending player immediately puts both hands in the air, which is always a sure sign of innocence.

   B) The player reacts to the "head injury" in a way that no other player ever does, such as actually going to the NHL-mandated quiet room.

   C) The team's media guide mentions that the player's off-season training partners are Peter Forsberg, Sean Avery, and Marcel Marceau.

   D) The borderline penalty he was reacting to was a delay of game call for shooting the puck over the glass.

2. **A high stick appears to make contact with a player's face. After he recovers from the initial contact, you can see that the player is:**

   A) Visibly shaken by the impact.

   B) Wiping away what appears to be blood.

   C) Wiping away what appears to be blood, while holding a handful of empty ketchup packets.

   D) Nonchalantly performing his own root canal on the bench in between shifts (Martin St. Louis only).

3. **A nearby microphone has picked up the audio of the play, and on the replay you can clearly hear:**

   A) The sound of a devastating impact that could not have been faked.

   B) The crowd murmuring in confusion over whether they'd witnessed a dive.

C) The player's teammate banging a clapperboard while yelling, "And, *action!*"

D) The player yelling, "NOOO!" as he dramatically falls to the ice in slow motion, which is odd since the replay was at regular speed.

4. **A player has been called for diving, but you suspect he may actually be innocent because:**

A) The replay seems to show legitimate contact right before he went down.

B) He just told the referee that he didn't dive, and hockey players never lie about that sort of stuff.

C) You're not sure how he would have gotten the ambulance driver and all the EMTs to play along like that.

D) He's one of those weird guys who insists on playing the game as if he has actual dignity and self-respect.

5. **After a big hit on the ice, Daniel Carcillo immediately grabs his face and begins flailing around on the ground. This makes you suspicious, because:**

A) The incident did not seem significant enough to warrant that much of a reaction.

B) Carcillo has a reputation for occasionally embellishing in an attempt to draw calls.

C) The other player immediately protested that he had barely touched him.

D) Carcillo's team isn't playing in that game, he's currently watching the game next to you in a bar 500 miles away, and he just dusted himself off and explained, "Sorry, force of habit."

6. **When all else fails, the easiest way to tell that a player is about to dive is by:**
   A) His attempt to make eye contact with the referee first.
   B) His use of his hands to brace himself for a fall.
   C) His old mattress that he dragged out onto the ice for a softer landing.
   D) His Canucks jersey.

You've completed the quiz! To determine whether the play in question was a dive, simply tally up all the answers from your quiz. Figure out which letter you chose most often, and then consult the scoring chart to find out . . . Oh, you know what, forget it. Just use this much simpler version, like every other hockey fan already does:

The player accused of diving plays for:
   A) My favorite team
   B) Some other team

Congratulations! You now have enough information to be convinced beyond any doubt whether you've witnessed a dive or not.

NO TIES ALLOWED

A History of the Shoot-out

The shoot-out has long been a topic that divides hockey fans. Many feel that it's an overly long and drawn-out skills competition, and a cheap gimmick that diminishes the emphasis on team play and tarnishes the integrity of the game. Others disagree, pointing out that it's actually not all that long.

But while the shoot-out may cause its share of controversy, there's no disputing that it has also created some unique hockey memories. Here's a sampling of some of the most indelible moments from the brief history of the NHL shoot-out:

February 13, 2008: After being given a rare shoot-out opportunity, a confused and frightened Tomas Kaberle spends the next forty-five minutes circling the offensive zone in a desperate attempt to find someone to pass to.

December 10, 2010: After telling Edmonton Oilers teammates that he was going to try something creative for a change, a disappointed Linus Omark is forced to switch to plan B after officials refuse to allow him to bring his ladder and bucket of confetti onto the ice.

November 2, 2009: Continuing his impressive streak as the only player in NHL history to be successful on every career shoot-out attempt, Gregory Campbell scores on his patented move of skating directly at the goaltender while yelling, "Get out of the way or my dad will suspend you!"

October 21, 2008: In a controversial effort to improve their chances of taking home two points, Maple Leafs coach Ron Wilson pulls Vesa Toskala before the shoot-out begins and replaces him with an old shoelace dangling from the crossbar.

November 27, 2010: Olli Jokinen streaks in across the blue line, kicks the puck up to his skates, and executes a breath-taking spinorama before being stopped by an arena worker who explains that game is already over and the Flames lost 7–1 in regulation.

March 24, 2010: Despite scoring on his first career attempt, Canadiens' defenseman P.K. Subban receives near-unanimous criticism from within the hockey community after he briefly cracks a facial expression.

October 25, 2005: Amid echoes of shots and clouds of gun smoke, the first shoot-out in Dallas Stars history resumes after the public address announcer sternly admonishes the Texas crowd because that's not the kind of "shoot-out" they meant and they know it.

April 11, 2009: The Flyers eliminate the Rangers from play-off contention on the season's final day, thanks to a move they call "glue the puck to the front of a stolen Zamboni and then run over Henrik Lundqvist while he's taking a drink from his water bottle."

November 3, 2009: Players begin to realize that the best way to score on Rick DiPietro is by coming in as slowly as possible, since given enough time he'll eventually keel over from some random injury, and you can just tap it into the open net.

January 1, 2008: After giving up the game-winning shoot-out goal to Sidney Crosby to end the first-ever outdoor Winter Classic, the Sabres' Ryan Miller comforts himself by telling reporters, "Oh well, at least I know that's the worst game-ending five-hole goal I'll ever give up to that guy on national television."

54

SO YOU WANT TO BE THE COMMISSIONER

The NHL's 1993 Job Application Form

The NHL will be celebrating an important anniversary on February 1, 2013: the twentieth anniversary of Gary Bettman's first day on the job as commissioner.

Whether hockey fans will also be celebrating is another matter. Bettman's reign has been nothing if not controversial, and has been marked by several notable successes (massively increased revenue, southern expansion, and unprecedented TV deals) as well as some definite failures (work stoppages, franchise instability, and the "dead puck" era).

It seems like Bettman's every move has been extensively examined and analyzed. Well, all except for one: his hiring. Sure, we all assume that it was the typical big-time executive hiring process, with a competitive recruitment, extensive interviews, and a high-stakes negotiation. But believe it or not, the entire process actually started with a simple application form.

And as luck would have it, DGB spies were able to track down the world's last remaining copy of the NHL's 1993 application form for potential commissioners.

Thank you for your interest in applying for the position of NHL commissioner. To help us learn more about potential candidates and ensure that we hire somebody who will be a great fit for this exciting opportunity, please complete the questionnaire below.

1. **Do you have any references from current or past employers?**

❏ Do not have any references available.

❏ Can provide phone numbers for reference checks.

❏ Can provide letters of recommendation signed by previous employers.

❏ Can provide a glowing recommendation from my current employer, David Stern, which he has assured me he is willing to deliver in person, since come to think of it he seems oddly enthusiastic about having me go and work for a league that competes directly with his.

2. **Why do you want to be NHL commissioner?**

❏ Getting tired of always hearing my name mentioned on ESPN.

❏ Have always wanted a chance to travel around North America learning about local bankruptcy laws.

❏ Enjoy posing awkwardly for photographs next to trophies that are taller than I am.

❏ Have heard you can be terrible at this job and still get to induct yourself into the Hockey Hall of Fame.

3. **While we have identified the need for our league to grow, we are obviously concerned about diluting the quality of our product due to too much expansion. How would you avoid this potential problem?**

❑ Limit geographic options by avoiding any areas that like hockey.

❑ Occasionally try going an entire year without adding any new teams, just to see what happens.

❑ Make the expansion draft format so unfair that nobody will even notice the new teams for years.

❑ Do not understand the words "too much expansion."

4. **Just curious, but, what is one plus one?**

❑ Two.

❑ Definitely two.

❑ Obviously two.

❑ Usually two. But every now and then, for no especially good reason, three.

5. **The first few years of the nineties were marked by fast, high-scoring, exciting games. How do you feel about the league's current style of play?**

❑ Current product is incredibly entertaining as is, but just in case, we should probably check back every ten years or so and see if anything has changed.

❑ To be honest, I find the nets kind of distracting; let's increase the size of goaltending equipment so that we never have to see them again.

❑ Pretty sure we could increase scoring even more if we randomly painted trapezoids behind the net for no reason.

❏ The NFL is super popular, and those guys are constantly grabbing and tackling each other; let's spend the next few years making that legal in hockey.

6. **Hey, you do realize that Canadians are going to complain about every single thing you do, no matter what, right?**

❏ Yep.

❏ Oh yeah.

❏ Definitely.

❏ What are "Canadians"?

7. **The NHL experienced its first league-wide work stoppage in 1992 when the players went on strike for ten days. If you became commissioner, what would be your approach to ensuring continued labor peace?**

❏ Lull the fans into a false sense of security by always letting a few seasons go by before another crippling work stoppage.

❏ Make sure that we never allow the cancellation of a full season to impact the league's popularity in the United States by first working hard to ensure that we have none.

❏ Just be glad we don't have to deal with a union head like that guy who's in charge of the MLB players association right now, because man, that dude is crazy!

❏ Oh, let's just say you won't have to worry about any ten-day work stoppages when I'm around. Muhahaha!

7. **Um, did you just cackle evilly in a written application form?**

❏ . . .

❏ Maybe.

8. **That's not even possible.**

❏   You cannot even begin to understand the powers I possess.

9. **What the . . . How did you just make it thunder and lightning outside?**

❏   MUHAHAHA!

10. **What time can you start on Monday morning?**

❏   I'll be there at 9:00 a.m.

❏   P.S. Make sure you paint a trapezoid behind my desk. I'll explain later.

55

THE NHL'S TOP-SECRET FLOW CHART FOR DEALING WITH SCANDALS

Over the years, the NHL has occasionally had to deal with unpleasant public relations problems. These sorts of things wouldn't happen in a perfect world, of course, but they're unavoidable for a business that operates under so much scrutiny.

Fans can probably recall some of the recent problems the league has had to face down: a suspicious clock malfunction in Los Angeles, Colin Campbell's email controversy, accusations of bias against referees. And let's not even get into the seemingly endless parade of owners who find themselves embroiled in various financial conflicts.

It would be easy for the league to try to sweep those sorts of problems under the rug. But to his credit, Gary Bettman doesn't let those close to him off the hook. Just like players and coaches, league officials are held to high standards and can face serious repercussions for stepping out of line. The league has a strict policy in place for ensuring accountability, and they follow it to the letter.

Here, thanks to my spies at the NHL head office, is the league's official document for handling high-level scandals and controversies.

NHL Scandal Flow Chart

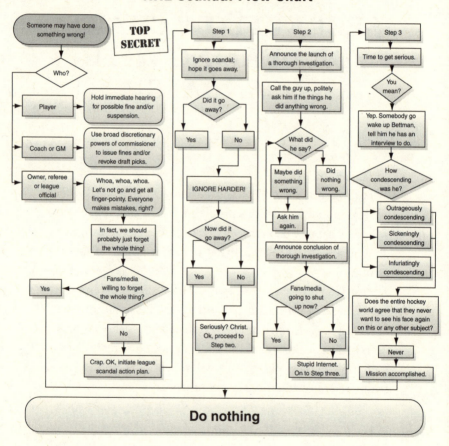

NOBODY REMEMBERS NUMBER TWO

A History of First Overall Draft Picks

The 2012 NHL Draft was a milestone for the league, marking the fiftieth year that teams had gathered to select players from among the available talent. The rules have changed over the years, with tweaks to everything from age limits to the number of rounds to the rules for determining the draft order. But one thing hasn't changed: Everyone wants to be number one.

So while a half-century of NHL drafts has seen thousands of players picked, only fifty can claim to have been taken at the top of their class. Some of those picks went on to stardom, championships, and a place in the Hall of Fame. Others, to put it kindly, wound up being disappointments.

Here's a look back at some of the players who have had the honor of being the first overall pick in the NHL draft:

1993: Alexandre Daigle, Ottawa Senators
His often-criticized prediction that nobody would ever remember who was picked second in that year's draft turned

out to be correct, given that many players who encountered
Chris Pronger during his career reported not remembering
anything at all afterwards.

1969: Réjean Houle, Montreal Canadiens

Scouts at the time would agree that the high-scoring winger
had never seen a goaltender that he couldn't deke out, or
beat on the glove side, or trade for a collection of spare parts
even though he was a first-ballot hall-of-famer in his prime.

2008: Steven Stamkos, Tampa Bay Lightning

Before even being officially selected, he was being marketed
with a series of billboards in Tampa Bay bearing the slogan
"Seen Stamkos?" Those were eventually replaced by billboards from the league's goaltenders reading "No, actually
we haven't. But does anyone know why that red light keeps
going on?"

2002: Rick Nash, Columbus Blue Jackets

After being selected, Nash shook hands with the Blue Jackets'
general manager, the head scout, and then a receiving line
of eight other guys who all introduced themselves as "your
future head coach for a season or two."

1996: Chris Phillips, Ottawa Senators

Phillips would go on to become known to fans and teammates
as Big Rig, which coincidentally was also the nickname of
the 2005 Sidney Crosby draft lottery machine.

1991: Eric Lindros, Quebec Nordiques

The consensus top pick famously refused to put on a Nordiques sweater and insisted that he would never play for the
franchise. Lindros faced withering criticism from fans and
media but refused to become discouraged, in what marked the
only known instance in his career of him keeping his head up.

2000: Rick DiPietro, New York Islanders
His frequently cited reputation for being injury plagued is grossly unfair, since the plague is occasionally treatable.

1971: Guy Lafleur, Montreal Canadiens
Lafleur's selection marked the fourth time the Canadiens had held the first overall pick since 1963, so they were obviously struggling through a perfectly normal decade-long rebuild, figure Edmonton fans.

2006: Erik Johnson, St. Louis Blues
He's a talented American defenseman who now plays for the Blue Jackets or maybe the Avalanche, according to the 90 percent of hockey fans who secretly don't know the difference between him and Jack Johnson.

1973: Denis Potvin, New York Islanders
The Hall of Fame defenseman went on to inspire Rangers fans to set a record for the all-time loudest "Potvin sucks" chant that would stand until 1996, when it was broken by Ron Hextall's orthodontist.

2004: Alexander Ovechkin, Washington Capitals
Advance scouting reports on the young Russian sniper were so overwhelmingly intimidating that the entire league decided to just take a year off rather than face him.

2007: Patrick Kane, Chicago Blackhawks
He is often compared to Eric Lindros in that they were both first overall picks who wore the number 88, although only one of them would find out what it's like to win the Stanley Cup in Philadelphia.

1984: Mario Lemieux, Pittsburgh Penguins
Lemieux declined to put on a Penguins jersey immediately after being chosen, partly due to a contract dispute with

Pittsburgh management, but mostly because it already had four Patrick Division defensemen hanging off of it.

1999: Patrick Stefan, Atlanta Thrashers

He is often referred to as the biggest draft bust of all time, but that's unfair because he was actually one of the more valuable players of the last decade, according to people who make hockey blooper videos on YouTube.

1983: Brian Lawton, Minnesota North Stars

Lawton was the first-ever American to be picked first overall, breaking down a barrier that would make it possible six years later for Mike Modano to become the first American to be picked first overall who is any good.

2011: Ryan Nugent-Hopkins, Edmonton Oilers

He was considered a perfect fit for the Oilers' system based on his time with the WHL's Red Deer Rebels, because he never played with any NHL defenseman there either.

1985: Wendel Clark, Toronto Maple Leafs

Although their scouts had prepared a long list of players who could potentially help the club, the Leafs eventually settled on Clark after every other prospect in the draft was mysteriously forced to retire that afternoon due to severe knuckle-shaped facial injuries.

HOW TO BECOME
AN IRONMAN

In sports, records are made to be broken. Or at least that's how it's supposed to work. But every now and then, somebody sets a record that seems untouchable. It's hard to imagine anyone ever beating Wayne Gretzky's 2,857 career points, or Teemu Selanne's 76 goals as a rookie. Glenn Hall's 502 consecutive starts as a goalie? Forget it.

And then there's Doug Jarvis. An excellent two-way forward in the seventies and eighties, Jarvis set the all-time NHL ironman record of 964 straight games. Steve Larmer looked like he may challenge the record for a time, but in the two decades since then no NHL player has managed to get close.

Will anyone ever again challenge Jarvis's mark? Maybe not. But if you're an NHL player hoping to start your own ironman streak, here are some common-sense tips that could help you get started on the road to the record book:

DO: Stay healthy by avoiding collisions that would increase your risk of suffering an injury.

DO NOT: Worry about collisions that carry absolutely no physical risk, such as running Ryan Miller in front of the entire Sabres roster.

DO: Feel confident that the NHL's recent changes to Rule 48 will drastically reduce the risk that you will suffer a serious head injury.

DO NOT: Attempt to actually understand how the league applies Rule 48, as this will cause a serious head injury.

DO: Follow the example of current league ironman Jay Bouwmeester by focusing all of your energy on training and conditioning that will allow you to continue your streak.

DO NOT: Allow yourself to become sidetracked by frivolous distractions, such as playing in the occasional postseason game.

DO: Follow league guidelines by taking and passing a comprehensive concussion screening test after suffering a hit to the head.

DO NOT: Feel pressured to take the test before you're ready; feel free to play in a few more games first, like everyone else does.

DO: Be aware of which opponents are out on the ice against you at all times.

DO NOT: Forget to casually brush the ice shavings from your uniform after uncurling from the fetal position once the referee assures you that, yes, Dion Phaneuf has finished his shift.

DO: Publicly commit yourself to following a strict diet of nutritious foods.

DO NOT: Let Gary Roberts overhear you saying that, since he'll make you actually do it.

DO: Reward yourself for all your hard work and dedication by taking advantage of some relaxation time at home, perhaps by surfing the internet or stretching out in front of the television.

DO NOT: Be surprised when the installation tech from the phone or cable company blindsides you in the side of the knee with a crescent wrench while muttering, "Go Leafs go."

DO: Hit the gym often to make sure you're in peak physical condition.

DO NOT: Bother working out any body parts other than upper body and lower body, since those are the only ones that anyone ever injures.

DO: Make sure you always wear the best and most modern equipment possible to protect important body parts like your elbows, shoulders, ankles, and shins.

DO NOT: Worry about also wearing something to protect your eyes, because hey, no point going overboard, right?

58

BEHIND THE SCENES AT NHL FAN TRAINING CAMP

OK, folks, can I get everyone's attention? Quiet in the back, please. Don't make me blow this whistle again. As you know, NHL team training camps have opened. And we thought this year it would be a good idea to do the same for all of you, the fans. So everyone take a knee and listen up.

Today we're going to go over some strategy for the coming season, diagram a few plays, and run a couple of drills. We may also have to send a few of you home. I know, I know, it won't be fun for me either, but what's a training camp without a few cuts? Everyone do your best and I'm sure you'll stick around.

OK, let's get started. First up is special teams. Now imagine your favorite team is on the power play. What are you fans going to be doing? Yes, that's right, you'll be yelling, "SHOOOOT" for the entire two minutes. Let's all practice that right now. Hey, good job, you guys are in mid-season form!

Hold up, I think someone back there had a question? Could you repeat that so everyone can hear? Shouldn't we wait for the players to get set up before we start yelling for them to shoot? OK, well, looks like we have our first cut. The rest of you work on your "SHOOOOT" while Mr. Smartypants here packs up his gear and heads for the nearest exit. It's over there next to the confused guy in the Thrashers jersey who really should have kept up with his hockey news.

For the rest of you, the next topic is fighting. Now this is going to be tricky. For years, this was the easiest part of being a fan. When a fight started, you stood up, screamed for a while, high-fived your buddy, and then sat down happy. But over the past few years we've been learning about the damage these fights can do, and it's not pretty.

So here's the new process, effective this season: stand up; start to cheer; realize you're not supposed to be cheering; look around to see if other fans are cheering; cheer halfheartedly so you don't seem like a wimp; sit down awkwardly; and be consumed by a haunting cognitive dissonance for the rest of the evening. OK, everyone got it? Begin!

Hmm . . . I guess this one is going to take some work.

You know what? Let's come back to that one. Instead, let's lighten the mood a little. Who's up for The Wave? Everybody ready? Three, two, one . . . go!

OK, that was actually a trick question. Everyone who stood up just now is cut. Thanks for coming out. We hear they may be having MLB tryouts next door.

While we're at it, the following fans are also cut: anyone who stands up to wave at a TV camera while holding a cell phone. Anyone who forwards stories they read on anonymous trade rumor websites. And anyone who makes jokes about how fat a player is while simultaneously weighing one hundred pounds more than that player.

OK, we've been at this for almost a half-hour, which means the Toronto Maple Leafs platinum season-ticket holders have finally started arriving. If anyone wants to pelt them with empty water bottles, be my guest. No batteries, Flyers fans!

All right, time for the "buying a team jersey" drill. When I blow the whistle, you sprint to the sales display and grab your favorite team's jersey. Then grab a match and light your paycheck on fire. Now sprint back, and see if you can put the jersey on and wear it for a few minutes before the team announces they're being replaced with brand new ones. Hmm. Nobody made it. Oh well, we can always work on . . .

OK, who threw that waffle?

Look, folks. While we admire your passion and even your creativity, one of the areas we really want to emphasize this year is only doing things that *make sense*. That means no throwing waffles or dressing up in a spandex bodysuit or buying Calgary Flames playoff tickets. Let's keep it in the real world.

What's that? Yes, of course you can still hide an octopus in your pants and then throw it at the national anthem singer. Like I said, we're only trying to get rid of the strange stuff.

OK, let's divide up for our last drill. This one is called "reacting rationally to seeing your team play poorly in one meaningless pre-season game." So everyone line up over there, next to the big pile of torches and pitchforks.

What's that? The Habs fans brought your own? Um . . . yeah. Well, that's why you guys are the greatest fans of all. No question about it. You guys are the best.

Please don't call 911.

SIGNS YOU MAY BE INJURY PRONE

Injuries are a hockey fact of life. By the time an NHL season has worn on for a few months, virtually everyone is fighting through some aches and pains. Many will play through them, while others have to miss games.

Of course, some players seem to find themselves in that latter group more often than others. Whether it's due to a reckless playing style, a refusal to play through pain, or just plain old bad luck, some players just always seem to be hurt. And once a player has earned a reputation for being injury prone, it can be a hard one to shake.

So if you're an NHL player wondering if you're hurt too often, read on for some possible signs that you may deserve the dreaded "injury prone" label.

- The two-paragraph section of the CBA dealing with the injured reserve mentions you by name fourteen times.

- Your hometown fans have booed Daniel Alfredsson ever since he mocked you by pretending to throw a broken femur into the stands.

- Every time your coach sends you onto the ice for a shift, the referee immediately gives him a match penalty for intent to injure.

- When he's angry at you, Zdeno Chara only bothers to guide you towards the general vicinity of the metal stanchion, instead of intentionally slamming you face-first into it.

- Every time somebody goes to hit you near the bench, the players and coaches all pull plastic sheeting over their heads like they're at a Gallagher show.

- Your scouting report describes you as "a chandelier, if it was made out of eggshells and *papier-mâché* by Rick DiPietro."

- When you were a kid, your parents used to always tell you, "Sticks and stones may break your bones, but words will only result in you being out day to day with a sprained medial collateral ligament."

- Any time somebody throws a body check against you in a game of *NHL 13* it makes your head bleed. Not your character's—yours.

- Instead of Don Cherry constantly calling you a flamingo on *Coach's Corner* because you lift one leg while blocking a shot, Don Cherry constantly calls you a flamingo on *Coach's Corner* because your knees bend the wrong way.

- While many players over the years have been mockingly described as being allergic to body contact, you're the only one who isn't allowed into the corners unless you're wearing your clip-on EpiPen pouch.

- Any time Raffi Torres skates towards you to deliver a potentially career-ending head shot, he pauses at the last second and then mumbles, "Oh, I guess somebody must have already got here."

- You spend every off-day visiting with as many children as possible at the local hospital, but eventually they all have to leave and go home.

- An ambulance follows you twenty-four hours a day, making you the first NHL player to have a red light flashing behind you at all times who wasn't a Maple Leafs goalie.

- Other players: often criticized for attempting to fight without first removing their helmet and visor. You: often criticized for attempting to fight without first removing your protective plastic bubble.

- Professional baseball players refer to you as "the toughest person we have ever seen."

60

INSIDE THE NHL'S LEGAL BRIEF ON THE 2011 NFL WORK STOPPAGE

Football fans had a rough off-season in 2011. The NFL was going through a messy labor dispute that would drag on for months, with many experts suggesting that a work stoppage could wipe out some or even all of the season.

In the end those dire predictions turned out to be wrong, with the two sides reaching an agreement that prevented any games from being lost. But not before the NHL managed to get involved in the protracted courtroom battle between the NFL and its players association, by filing a legal brief urging a judge to side with the owners.

The move caught many observers off guard, and raised an obvious question: What sort of insight could the NHL really have to offer into football's problems? Plenty, as it turns out. I managed to obtain a top-secret copy of the NHL's brief, and found that it contains detailed advice that NFL owners no doubt found invaluable. Here's a selection of highlights from the filing:

- The cover page of the document has a note, in what appears to be NFL commissioner Roger Goodell's handwriting, that reads: "Should I have heard of these guys?"

- The brief contains a lengthy section titled: "How to keep a straight face if the players start to swear that they'll never accept a hard salary cap."

- The league includes a helpful suggestion that the NFL consider generating some publicity by holding an outdoor game at a football stadium.

- Under the heading "Typo Alert," NHL officials write: "Couldn't help but notice that you keep claiming you make several billion dollars a year off of your TV deal. Silly NFL, 'million' is spelled with an 'm'!"

- At the request of NHL officials, the brief includes the following note: "Hey, can you ask your referees where they get those microphones that actually work during crucial calls?"

- Three-quarters of the document's pages are spent trying to explain the NHL's exact policy on head shots.

- The brief includes a note from Mike Murphy that reads: "The guys in your replay room must be blind, because somebody scores using a distinctive kicking motion in, like, every single game."

- A copy of Gary Bettman's résumé was "accidentally" slipped in between the first two pages.

- At one point, the NHL writes: "That little silver football thing you guys have is adorable, but give us a call if you ever decide to move up to giving out big-boy trophies."

- The league strongly encourages owners in other sports to stand firm in labour disputes, at one point noting: "In fact, if both the NFL and NBA wanted to just cancel the next several seasons, we'd be totally fine with that."

- The brief includes a section titled: "A detailed guide to televising a draft without letting your announcers ruin the suspense of every pick ten seconds before it's announced."

- In incredibly tiny type at the bottom of the last page, the document includes the words: "By reading this brief, you agree that you are now the proud new owner of the Phoenix Coyotes."

- The brief concludes with this sentence: "Despite the many differences between our two leagues, at the very least we can all come together and agree that the Panthers suck."

61

AN IN-DEPTH COMPARISON

Sidney Crosby vs. Alexander Ovechkin

It all seemed so perfect. Coming out of the lockout, the NHL found itself with two brand new stars. Despite different personalities, Sidney Crosby and Alexander Ovechkin were both young and marketable. When the Capitals and Penguins both quickly developed into Stanley Cup contenders, it seemed like the league had finally found a head-to-head battle with the potential to attract a new generation of fans. What could possibly go wrong?

Everything, it now seems. Crosby's battle with concussion symptoms has been well documented, forcing him to miss most of the 2011–12 season. Meanwhile, Ovechkin often seems to have lost the spark that made him dominant. One can't-miss star now seems ordinary when he takes the ice, while the other spends most of his time in the trainer's room.

Maybe this is just a short-term detour in what will still be a long and entertaining rivalry. Or maybe we've already seen the best these two have to offer. Either way, it appears the two stars will be linked for years to come. Here's a comparison of two talented and popular young players who were once viewed as the league's future, and hopefully will be again.

Alexander Ovechkin: Has been known to get angry with his coach while on the bench and shout obscenities.

Sidney Crosby: Has been known to get angry with his coach while on the bench and shout, "I'm just going to go out there and give 110 percent!" since that's all he's programmed to ever say.

Sidney Crosby: Wears jersey #87, signifying his year of birth.

Alexander Ovechkin: Wears jersey #8, signifying the number of goals he needs to score in any given game before he won't automatically be blamed if the Capitals lose.

Alexander Ovechkin: Has been invited to throw out the ceremonial first pitch at games for the Washington Nationals and Baltimore Orioles.

Sidney Crosby: Would probably be thrilled to do the same if Pittsburgh ever managed to get a professional baseball team.

Sidney Crosby: Has had the opportunity to hone his acting ability in commercials for brands like Reebok and Tim Hortons.

Alexander Ovechkin: Has had the opportunity to hone his acting ability every time his coach starts yelling about maybe back-checking once in a while and he has to pretend that he's listening.

Alexander Ovechkin: Has occasionally found himself in trouble with the league due to questionable hits against defenseless opponents.

Sidney Crosby: Would never check a defenseless opponent in a dangerous manner because he is classy and respects the game and Matt Cooke usually gets there first.

Sidney Crosby: May one day come to be viewed as a cautionary example who taught a generation of fans a valuable lesson about the dangers of head injuries.

Alexander Ovechkin: May one day come to be viewed as a cautionary example who taught a generation of fans a valuable lesson about the dangers of thinking it's a good idea for guys to get lower-back tattoos.

Alexander Ovechkin: Is so good at anticipating the flow of the game that he can often react to an incoming pass attempt before the puck has even left his teammate's stick.

Sidney Crosby: Is so good at anticipating the flow of the game that he can often react to an opposing player's attempted body check by falling down before he's even touched.

Sidney Crosby: Has had one fifty-goal season so far, and given his injury concerns experts admit they have no idea how many more he may have over the course of his career.

Alexander Ovechkin: Rather than cause all sorts of confusion, was apparently considerate enough to get all of his fifty-goal seasons out of the way early.

Alexander Ovechkin: Owns the hockey world's record for the most Twitter followers, with 400,000.

Sidney Crosby: Owns the hockey world's record for the most MySpace friends, with nine.

Sidney Crosby: Die-hard Pittsburgh fans will eagerly tell you that he's following in the footsteps of legendary Penguins from past generations, like Mario Lemieux, Ron Francis, and Paul Coffey.

Alexander Ovechkin: Die-hard Washington fans will eagerly tell you that he's following in the footsteps of legendary Capitals from past generations, before trailing off, furrowing their brows, and eventually changing the subject.

Alexander Ovechkin: Despite his flashy on-ice personality, is known to dress casually off the ice and rarely calls attention to himself with gaudy accessories.

Sidney Crosby: In contrast to the classy Ovechkin, has been known to walk out of the arena wearing a giant diamond-studded ring or a gold medallion around his neck.

MAKE HIS
HEAD BLEED

A History of the NHL
in Pop Culture

Let's be honest: Despite a dedicated following in Canada and several American cities, even the most die-hard fan would have to admit that hockey is, for the most part, still a niche sport in most of the United States. Fans have learned to embrace the sport's status as an underdog, and to appreciate the rare opportunities to see it break through to a larger audience.

Maybe that's why we get so excited when we catch a glimpse of the NHL in popular culture. Whether it's an unexpected cameo by a well-known player, a passing mention of a team, or even just a logo flashing by in the background, hockey fans tend to remember the moments when their favorite sport shows up in a popular movie or television show.

Here are some notable examples of hockey crossing over, however briefly, into the mainstream:

1996: The movie *Swingers* features a scene in which a character playing a video game vows to "make Wayne Gretzky's head bleed for super-fan number 99 over here." Because the movie involves an illegal play, blood, and Wayne Gretzky, Kerry Fraser never sees it.

2000: Brendan Shanahan makes a brief appearance playing a state trooper in the movie *Me, Myself and Irene.* He will later abandon plans for a post-playing career in Hollywood, explaining that he'd prefer to take on a job where there would be more critics.

1986: NHL players such as Peter Zezel and Steve Thomas make cameos in the hit movie *Youngblood*, an inspiring story of a young hockey player portrayed by Rob Lowe who overcomes the odds to become a superstar despite apparently never having been taught how to skate.

1987: The sitcom *Cheers* introduces popular character Eddie LeBec, setting a standard for the best comedy performance by a Boston Bruins goaltender that will remain unchallenged until the day Tim Thomas discovers Facebook.

1981: Wayne Gretzky appears on the soap opera *The Young and the Restless.* In a bit of ironic foreshadowing, he plays a character that dumps his longtime love for a richer, more exciting one from Los Angeles, but then never gets her a ring.

1994: Cam Neely makes an appearance in *Dumb and Dumber*, a documentary about the Vancouver Canucks scouts who thought it would be a good idea to trade him for Barry Pederson.

1997: Noted Toronto fan Mike Myers pays tribute to the Maple Leafs in the hit movie *Austin Powers: International Man of Mystery* by including characters named after Nikolai Borschevsky ("General Borschevsky"), Doug Gilmour ("Commander Gilmour"), and Harold Ballard ("Dr. Evil").

1977: Minor league forward and future NHL head coach Bruce Boudreau has a few seconds of screen time in the cult classic *Slap Shot*, in what was originally scheduled to be a leading role until censors forced the film's producers to cut out any scenes where he swore.

2010: The romantic comedy *She's Out of My League* features a scene where the main characters watch the Islanders play the Penguins before passionately embracing, in what turns out to just be a futile attempt to drown out the sound of Mario Lemieux complaining.

1995: An episode of *Seinfeld* features a die-hard hockey fan who paints his face in Devils colors, marking the last-known instance of NBC being aware that there are any hockey teams besides the Rangers, Flyers, and Penguins.

1987: The popular family sitcom *Full House* includes the lovable character Uncle Joey, a die-hard Red Wings fan who often wears the team's jersey. Producers will later consider spinning off Uncle Joey into his own Red Wings–themed show called *Pretty Close to a Full House So Let's Just Ignore All Those Empty Seats Up There Even Though It's a Playoff Game.*

1996: Adam Sandler's character in *Happy Gilmore* dons a Boston Bruins jersey before being pummeled in a fist fight by elderly game show host Bob Barker, who will admit to being confused fifteen years later when he suddenly starts getting contract offers from the Vancouver Canucks.

1997: Tomas Kaberle is fired from his role working on the re-released version of the original *Star Wars* after George Lucas realizes that there aren't enough special effects in the world to make him shoot first.

2012: Sean Avery appears as a guest judge on a modeling reality show called *Project Runway*, which is not to be confused with his appearance on the ice for any shift against a legitimate NHL heavyweight, which was called *Project Run Away*.

1998: During certain broadcasts of the network television show *The NHL on Fox*, some viewers swear that if you look very closely in the background behind where the giant robots are fighting each other with lasers you could actually see a hockey game being played.

63

WHEN A DAY WITH THE STANLEY CUP GOES WRONG

Every hockey player dreams of getting to spend a day with the Stanley Cup. For many, it's the ultimate opportunity to share their success with their family, friends, and hometown fans.

For others, the day can be . . . less successful. Take Boston Bruins forward Nathan Horton, who had planned to enjoy his 2011 day with the Cup in his hometown of Dunnville, Ontario. But the Cup missed its flight, and Horton had to appear in front of the assembled fans empty-handed.

The Cup did eventually arrive for a shortened appearance at the event, and an embarrassed Horton apologized to the crowd. But he shouldn't have felt bad. Despite all the feel-good stories we're used to hearing during the summer, Horton was actually just the latest in a long line of NHL players to have problems with the world's most famous trophy.

Here's a look back at some past champions who had their day with the Cup go badly:

1999: Brett Hull is half an hour late returning the Cup in violation of the long-enforced twenty-four-hour limit, but everyone agrees to just pretend that rule doesn't exist rather than make a big deal out of it.

2001: Whitby's Adam Foote is disappointed after spending the entire day showing off the Cup to hockey fans in nearby Toronto, only to discover that none of them recognize it.

2007: Officials are forced to explain to a disappointed crowd in Fort McMurray that, yes, it was easily the biggest goal of his career and, yes, it will go down in the record books as the Stanley Cup winner, but no, Chris Phillips still isn't getting a day with the Cup.

1996: The Cup leaves North America for the first time when it travels to Sweden with Peter Forsberg, then proceeds to spend the rest of the summer annoying everyone by being unable to make up its mind about whether it wants to return.

2003: Joe Nieuwendyk brings the Cup to his alma mater at Cornell University, drawing such a huge crowd that the school is forced to cancel that day's scheduled lecture entitled "A detailed theoretical model of why anyone who becomes a general manager someday should probably trade their franchise player at the deadline if he's obviously planning to sign as a free agent with the Rangers that summer."

2004: Martin St. Louis's day with the Cup is ruined when he accidentally tumbles into the bowl and spends the rest of the afternoon adorably squeaking for somebody to come and lift him out.

1995: After winning the franchise's first championship, members of the New Jersey Devils save everyone time by just going ahead and engraving "A bunch of boring guys playing the trap and making you hate hockey" into the Cup's next ten years' worth of panels.

1994: While spending his sixth day with the Cup in the last ten years, Mark Messier realizes he's really getting tired of all these championships and resolves to sign his next free agent contract with a franchise that has no hope of ever winning one.

2010: After several intense hours, Jonathan Toews wins the staring contest when the Cup blinks first.

2009: As he sits alone in front of a giant cake in a balloon-filled gymnasium with a party hat tilted sadly to one side, Joe Thornton begins to realize that fans aren't really interested in helping you celebrate your day with the Presidents' Trophy.

1991: The Cup is famously left at the bottom of Mario Lemieux's swimming pool during a players' party after nobody goes in to retrieve it, marking the only time in recent NHL history that nobody on the Pittsburgh Penguins is willing to dive.

64

BREAKING DOWN THE BATTLES

Inside Canada's Provincial Rivalries

The long-rumored return of the NHL to Quebec City has hockey fans thinking ahead to a rekindling of one of hockey's greatest rivalries. The Battle of Quebec between the Montreal Canadiens and Quebec Nordiques raged memorably through the 1980s, stirring up passion that went beyond mere hockey games to become a symbol for a province's political and cultural divides.

Of course, Quebec isn't the only Canadian province to feature an intense rivalry. The Battle of Alberta was every bit as hard fought at its peak, and more recently the Battle of Ontario produced its share of dramatic moments.

But which provincial battle burned the brightest? Let's take a closer look at all three of Canada's greatest hockey rivalries.

Familiarity

Battle of Alberta: The teams played each other so often that fans knew the other side's roster by heart.

Battle of Quebec: The teams played each other so often that bench-clearing brawls would sometimes occur before the game had even begun.

Battle of Ontario: The teams played each other so often that Bob Cole came really close to learning a few of the Senators' names.

Playoff predictability

Battle of Quebec: You could always expect a hard-fought series with plenty of bad blood.

Battle of Ontario: You could always expect a close-checking series in which goaltending would be the deciding factor.

Battle of Alberta: You could always expect the series to end with an Edmonton player scoring the winning goal.

Star players in the spotlight

Battle of Alberta: Wayne Gretzky would look across at the Flames and know that he was in for a difficult game.

Battle of Ontario: Daniel Alfredsson would look across at the Maple Leafs and realize that he'd need to someday beat them in the playoffs to cement his legacy.

Battle of Quebec: Patrick Roy would look across at the Nordiques and think, "Man, it sure would be fun to win a bunch of Stanley Cups with those guys someday."

Memorable overtime moment

Battle of Quebec: Dale Hunter's overtime winner in 1982 is memorable for the momentary confusion over whether the puck had actually crossed the goal line.

Battle of Alberta: Theo Fleury's overtime winner in 1991 is memorable for his enthusiastic rink-long celebration.

Battle of Ontario: Cory Cross's overtime winner in 2001 is memorable for the sound of 19,000 Maple Leafs fans simultaneously mumbling, "Wait a second, Cory Cross actually scored a goal?"

Behind the bench

Battle of Ontario: Senators coach Jacques Martin was constantly reviewing game film in search of opportunities to improve his players' defensive positioning.

Battle of Alberta: Oilers coach Glen Sather was constantly looking for ways to keep his star players motivated as they chased yet another championship.

Battle of Quebec: Nordiques coach Michel Bergeron was constantly wondering why Dale Hunter kept asking him whether he had any tips on coaching overpaid Russian head cases.

Clutch player

Battle of Alberta: No matter how bad the situation seemed, Oilers fans never stopped believing that Mark Messier would come through when they needed him.

Battle of Quebec: No matter how bad the situation seemed, Nordique fans never stopped believing that Michel Goulet would come through when they needed him.

Battle of Ontario: No matter how bad the situation seemed, Maple Leafs fans never stopped believing that Patrick Lalime would come through when they needed him.

Notable villain

Battle of Alberta: A Dave Semenko sucker punch on Tim Hunter very nearly caused both benches to empty.

Battle of Quebec: Louis Sleigher's sucker punch on Jean Hamel helped to touch off a brawl that actually did cause both benches to empty.

Battle of Ontario: Darcy Tucker was a classy player who felt so strongly about making sure the benches didn't empty that he would set a positive example by occasionally randomly leaping into one.

Red Wings connection

Battle of Ontario: Toronto's Curtis Joseph went on to become a popular player in Detroit when he chose to sign there as a free agent.

Battle of Alberta: Calgary's Mike Vernon went on to become a popular player in Detroit when he helped them win their first Stanley Cup in over forty years.

Battle of Quebec: Montreal's Claude Lemieux went on to become a popular player in Detroit, we assume, since every time he played there the Red Wings players would line up in the parking lot to personally greet him.

Superstars switching sides

Battle of Quebec: Canadiens' legend Guy Lafleur finished his career with a brief stint with the Nordiques.

Battle of Alberta: Oilers' legend Grant Fuhr finished his career with a brief stint with the Flames.

Battle of Ontario: Maple Leafs' legend Mats Sundin did not finish his career with a brief stint with the Senators, yet. Although the idea only occurred to him a few years ago, so let's all give him some time to make up his mind.

Potential return of the post-season rivalry

Battle of Quebec: An existing franchise moving to Quebec City could set the table for the province's first post-season battle in twenty years.

Battle of Ontario: With both teams rebuilding and featuring talented young rosters, a return of their post-season rivalry seems inevitable.

Battle of Alberta: Uh . . . any chance we could interest you in a *pre*-season rivalry?

WELCOME TO THE DOGHOUSE

A History of Coach vs. Player Feuds

There are two things that every NHL team needs if it's going to contend for a championship: a superstar player, and a great coach. Of course, it also helps if that coach and that player get along.

That didn't seem to be the case in Washington during the 2011–12 season. After Bruce Boudreau benched him during a crucial shift late in the game, Alexander Ovechkin appeared to react to the news by barking some well-chosen obscenities in the coach's direction. While the two later made an effort to seem like they were on the same page, that didn't stop fans and the media from speculating about a rift that may have helped lead to Boudreau's eventual firing and the Capitals' disappointing regular season.

An overreaction? Probably, because this sort of thing actually happens all the time. The NHL has a long history of disagreements between superstar players and their coaches, and many of them were far more serious than a few expletives uttered in the heat of the moment.

Here's a look back at ten other notable star vs. coach feuds in NHL history:

November 2003: An enraged Scott Stevens accuses Devils' coach Pat Burns of not being a first ballot hall-of-famer, before later apologizing and admitting that could only happen in a world where the selection committee was made up entirely of idiots.

February 1978: Bruins' defenseman Brad Park finds himself in the doghouse after coach Don Cherry realizes his name is completely impossible to mispronounce.

December 2008: Team captain Daniel Alfredsson requests a one-hour meeting with the head coach to discuss his declining ice time, but eventually gets tired of having to start over again every fifteen minutes whenever Bryan Murray hires someone new.

February 2001: Vincent Lecavalier is momentarily confused by the sight of a red-faced John Tortorella gesturing furiously while screaming obscenities at him, before veteran teammates reassure him it's just how the coach says good morning.

March 1998: Canucks coach Mike Keenan calls captain Mark Messier into his office to explain that, while the league's policy on gambling may be open to interpretation, he still needs to stop constantly trying to bet his teammates that they can't eat just one.

October 2010: The Islanders' attempts to send a message to the rest of the team by scratching their highest-paid player prove fruitless when they are unable to figure out how to bench Alexei Yashin's buyout.

April 1987: A concerned Jari Kurri tells Oilers coach Glen Sather that while he agrees the team's unquestioned dominance does result in them occasionally becoming complacent, he's still not sold on this whole "let's occasionally score into our own net just to make it more challenging" plan.

March 2006: A confused Mike Babcock begins to wonder why Brendan Shanahan won't accept anything he says unless it's accompanied by an awkward videotaped explanation.

January 2009: After an obscenity-filled exchange ends with head coach Wayne Gretzky suggesting he go meet with the new assistant, Shane Doan thinks about how much he appreciates being able to air his grievances and makes a mental note to apologize for his harsh tone. He then briefly wonders why the new assistant coach looks so much like Dave Semenko holding a crowbar.

January 1996: In an effort to get him to take on more of a leadership role, Bruins head coach Steve Kasper humiliates Cam Neely by benching him during a nationally televised game. To his credit, Neely responds positively the very next day by delivering a moving eulogy at the funeral of Steve Kasper.

January 2006: Penguins coach Michel Therrien grows frustrated when star player Mario Lemieux repeatedly responds to criticism by saying, "Hey, good point. Maybe you should call up the owner and let him know."

March 1993: Pat Burns shows that he doesn't play favorites when he briefly removes a slumping Doug Gilmour from the team's first line, although Gilmour does remain on the second, third, and fourth lines, both power play units, and the penalty kill.

July 1995: In an effort to send a message to the rest of the team, you briefly demote Jeremy Roenick from the first line during a game of *NHL 95* even though it makes your big brother punch you in the shoulder and call you a spaz.

January 1994: After Pavel Bure complains yet again about a lack of chemistry with center Cliff Ronning, a frustrated Pat Quinn vows that if he ever coaches another European franchise player, he just won't ever bother giving him any good linemates at all.

KNOW YOUR SPORTS
The NHL vs. UFC

Mixed martial arts is one of the fastest-growing sports in the world. The top fighters are becoming international celebrities, TV ratings are high, and pay-per-view events bring in millions of dollars. And these days, many hockey fans are already watching popular MMA promotions such as the UFC.

But others may not be sure what all the hype is about. If you fall into the latter category, here's a hockey fan's guide to how the UFC stacks up with the NHL:

UFC: A fighter signals that he has lost his will to win and no longer wishes to compete by "tapping out."
NHL: A player signals that he has lost his will to win and no longer wishes to compete by signing a contract extension with the Edmonton Oilers.

UFC: A hyper-extended elbow with a broken arm can be the result of a competitor not tapping out quickly after the successful application of an armbar.

NHL: A hyper-extended elbow with a broken arm is an acceptable reason to miss one or two shifts during the play-offs while the trainer tapes it up.

UFC: "The World's Most Dangerous Man" was the nickname of UFC hall-of-famer Ken Shamrock.

NHL: "The World's Most Dangerous Man" is what Flyers fans call whoever is starting in net for that night's playoff game.

UFC: There is a common misconception that the sport is a vicious free-for-all where anything goes no matter how brutal, when in fact it is governed by a clear set of strictly enforced rules.

NHL: There is a common misconception that the sport is governed by a clear set of strictly enforced rules.

UFC: Ground and pound is a fighting style that aims to take an opponent to the mat and then employ a striking attack from a dominant position.

NHL: Ground and pound is Bruce Boudreau's answer to the question "What is your favorite type of beef, and how much of it have you smuggled into the arena tonight in your pockets?"

UFC: If a match does not end in regulation time, it goes to the judges' decision; in especially even and hard-fought contests, the fight can be declared a draw.

NHL: The league knows that real sports fans don't enjoy ties, and fans would be much happier if the UFC moved to deciding matches with a rock-paper-scissors contest.

UFC: The action takes place inside a caged structure called an octagon, which many critics have called the most dangerous structure in all of sports.

NHL: The action takes place inside a rink, which has been carefully designed to ensure the safety of all—oh good God look out for that stanchion!

UFC: If a girl in a bikini holds up the number one to the crowd, it signifies that the first round of a fight is about to begin.

NHL: If a guy in a Bruins jersey holds up the number one to the crowd, it signifies that his glove got stuck, he says.

UFC: Competitors know that it's time to start throwing punches when they hear those four words: "Let's get it on!"

NHL: Competitors know that it's time to start throwing punches when they hear those four words: "Hello, I'm Patrick Kaleta."

UFC: Fans are encouraged to watch *The Ultimate Fighter*, a made-for-TV production that is occasionally entertaining despite the results holding little actual importance.

NHL: Same concept, but they call it "the regular season."

UFC: Canadian star Georges St-Pierre employs a methodical style that is highly effective but is often criticized for not producing exciting or dramatic moments.

NHL: Georges St-Pierre has been offered the head coaching job in New Jersey.

UFC: Popular commentator Joe Rogan is also one of his country's best-known stand-up comedians.

NHL: Popular commentator Don Cherry is also one of his country's best-known stand-up comedians, although he doesn't seem to realize it.

UFC: A "choke" is a legal manoeuvre in which a competitor cuts off his opponent's air supply in order to secure a quick submission.

NHL: Insert your own Vancouver Canucks joke here.

A HOCKEY FAN'S GUIDE TO MODERN TV TECHNOLOGY

Televised hockey has seen some big changes in technology over the past few years. The days of struggling to find the puck on a tiny screen are over, now that most games are broadcast in high-definition, and some networks have even experimented with broadcasting games in 3D.

That's all great news if you have a state-of-the-art television. But plenty of hockey fans don't. And in fact, some are still watching the game on old-fashioned sets without any of the bells and whistles that so many others now take for granted.

My guess is that many of those late adopters are at least considering an upgrade to a more modern system. And if you're one of them, I'm here to help with this handy guide to get a hockey fan up and running with the latest television technology.

Getting started

First step: Go buy an expensive television and home entertainment system, bring it home, and hook it up. Go ahead, I'll wait here.

Are you back? Great. Let's make sure you're ready for some hockey. First, press the power button on one of the seven remote controls you now own. No, not that one. The one that's kind of grayish. No, the *other* one that's kind of grayish. You know what? Just hit the power buttons on all of them. Good, we're ready to get started.

High-definition television

To hook up your high-def TV, follow these steps:

1. First, tune your television to your favorite sports channel so you can see what the broadcasters look like in standard definition.
2. Next, locate the HDMI cable and plug it into the back of your TV.
3. Now check the screen and see what the broadcasters look like in high-definition.
4. Finally, yank the HDMI cable out of the television and throw it out the window before collapsing on the ground, clawing at your eyes in horror.

Watching television in 3D

If you've purchased a 3D set, put on your special glasses and wait for something to be projected directly towards the screen. If you're watching a made-for-3D movie, this will happen every few seconds. If you're watching anything else, this will happen never.

Helpful hint: When watching hockey in 3D, it's probably a good idea to look away from the screen any time James Wisniewski starts getting angry.

Stereo sound

Your new entertainment system will feature stereo sound that delivers a much richer experience. Set up the various speakers in strategic locations around the room, and soon you'll be enjoying the sound of your friends telling you that you didn't put them in the right place.

You'll also be able to hear enhanced audio during hockey games, such as hits rattling off the glass, players calling for passes, and enhanced crowd noise. (Please note: Crowd noise not available for games broadcast from the Air Canada Centre.)

The personal video recorder

A personal video recorder (or PVR) is a device that allows you to pause, record, fast-forward, and rewind live television. While it can be used for any type of programing, it's especially useful for sports fans who want to record games to watch later.

Your system will come with a handy on-screen guide that will make the process easy. Scroll through the menu to find the game you want to record. Notice that the guide is helpfully set to record the game from 7:00 p.m. to 9:30 p.m., which is fine since nobody really wants to see the end of the third period anyway.

When it's time to watch the game you've recorded, you can fast-forward until you see something interesting happening. Then you can fast-forward past that while you try to remember where the rewind button is. Then you can rewind too far and miss it again. Then you can accidentally press the "live" button, skip directly to the end of the game, see the final score, and throw your remote control out the window. Don't worry; you still have six more.

Helpful hint: Remember to feel slightly guilty about fast-forwarding through the national anthem.

The Blu-ray player

A Blu-ray player is a device that allows Edmonton Oilers fans to watch movies during the playoffs.

Troubleshooting

Still having problems? Try some of these fixes to common issues:

Problem: I recorded my favorite team's game and decided to watch all their goals, fights and big hits, but I ended up just fast-forwarding and fast-forwarding until the game was over.

Solution: Stop cheering for the New York Islanders.

Problem: My TV is stuck on an image of Sidney Crosby, and the Penguins aren't even playing in this game.

Solution: You have accidentally switched over to an NBC broadcast.

Problem: I'm pressing my remote control's mute button, but the announcer just keeps getting louder.

Solution: You are attempting to mute Pierre McGuire. Nobody can mute Pierre McGuire.

Problem: The picture starts out sharp and clear for the opening face-off, but becomes increasingly blurry as the game goes on until it is almost impossible to tell what's happening.

Solution: You are a Toronto Maple Leafs fan. Try not to drink so much during the game.

BEHIND THE SCENES AT THE MATT COOKE SUSPENSION HEARING

Start a conversation with a hockey fan about the game's most hated players, and it won't take long before Matt Cooke's name comes up. The controversial Penguins winger has racked up a long list of suspensions and controversies, and is often cited as the poster child for everything that's wrong with the NHL.

Is that fair? Not entirely. After all, Cooke actually cleaned up his act for much of the 2011–12 season. But that was only after he'd appeared to run out of chances. His elbow to the head of Ryan McDonagh near the end of the 2010–11 season was so flagrant that even Pittsburgh owner Mario Lemieux spoke out against it, and the league handed out an uncharacteristically lengthy suspension.

What was it about Cooke that had even Colin Campbell, often criticized for being too lenient, ready to lower the boom? A transcript of Cooke's suspension hearing offers some clues.

Scene: The NHL's head office, inside a window-lined boardroom with "Department of Supplemental Discipline" written on the door. Colin Campbell, Mike Murphy, and Gary Bettman sit at one end of a large table, with Matt Cooke and Mario Lemieux at the other.

Colin Campbell: Hi, Matt. Welcome to the hearing. Did you have any trouble finding a parking spot?

Matt Cooke: Nah, I just parked out front in the "Reserved for Matt Cooke" space.

Campbell: Great. So I've watched the replay of this Ryan McDonagh hit a dozen times. It sure looks like you're intentionally targeting a defenseless opponent with a flagrant elbow to the head. How can you possibly defend your actions?

Cooke: Um . . . it was an accident?

Campbell: An accident.

Cooke *(hesitates)*: Yes?

A long pause. Campbell stares at Cooke intently before finally breaking the silence.

Campbell: Great, well thanks for clearing that up. Zero games. Sorry for troubling you.

Campbell and Murphy begin gathering up their papers and prepare to leave the room. Cooke looks around in confusion.

Gary Bettman: Uh, everyone? Could we hold on just a second? Maybe we could talk about this one a little more?

Campbell and Murphy stop in the doorway.

Campbell: Well, sure, I guess. If you want to.

Bettman: You know, just since we have the room booked and all.

Campbell *(returning to his seat)*: OK. Well, since I've already subjected Matt to in-depth questioning . . . Mario, do you have anything to say?

Mario Lemieux: Do I have to?

Campbell: Yes.

Lemieux *(sighing)*: Fine. Look, he's on my team. He's one of my players, technically. So . . . you know . . . don't suspend him, I guess.

Campbell: That's very helpful, thanks.

Lemieux: I need to leave now.

Lemieux bolts out the door.

Campbell: Thanks, Mario. Our next witness is scheduled to be . . . Hmm, what does it say on my sheet here? "A world-renowned and completely impartial hockey expert, named . . . Dr. Wario Mellieux."

A man who looks oddly like Mario Lemieux wearing a moustache made out of duct tape walks into the room.

Campbell: Dr. Mellieux, your thoughts?

Mellieux: Matt Cooke is an abomination, a scumbag, an embarrassment, everything that's wrong with the game. I hate him. He should be banned for life.

Cooke: Dude . . .

Mellieux: And also, he shouldn't count against the salary cap while he's suspended.

They're interrupted by a figure poking his head in the door.

Trevor Gillies: You wanted to see me, Colin?

Campbell: Uh . . . no.

Gillies (*looking down at a newspaper with headline reading "Hockey's biggest cheap-shot artist facing suspension yet again"*): Oh. Oops, my mistake.

Campbell: No problem, Trevor. Talk to you in a few weeks.

Gillies: Sure thing. By the way, whoever's driving the Mercedes-Benz with the MARIO66 vanity plates, I smashed into it from behind. Sorry.

Mellieux: Son of a . . .

Delivery guy (*entering room*): OK, who ordered the large pizza with extra cheese and—

Matt Cooke leaps to his feet and begins elbowing the delivery guy repeatedly in the head.

Bettman: Matt?

Cooke: Oops. My bad. Sorry, everyone. Force of habit.

Bettman: Don't worry about it. Hey, at least you didn't slam his face into a stanchion!

Zdeno Chara (*poking his head through a window*): I heard that!

Cooke: Aren't we on the third floor?

Bettman: Never mind that. Look, Matt, your hit was very dangerous, but you're here to defend yourself. So go ahead, tell us why we shouldn't throw the book at you.

Cooke: Look, I know I've made mistakes. I'm a physical player and, yes, I step over the line sometimes. But so do lots of players, and most of them don't get big suspensions.

Campbell: Exactly. I recently went easy on Dany Heatley and Brad Marchand, and I didn't suspend Chara at all.

Mellieux (*under his breath*): Or that jerk who took out Marc Savard.

Campbell: Shush. The point is, plenty of players do dirty things without getting suspended. Why start getting tough now, right?

Cooke: Exactly! I mean, honestly, is hitting one guy in the head really any more dirty that smashing a guy in the face repeatedly with your elbow pad, the way Gregory Campbell did a few games ago against Montreal?

The room immediately goes silent.

Cooke: Uh . . . I mean . . .

Everyone is too horrified to speak.

Campbell *(calmly)*: I'm sorry, Matt, could you repeat that? Any more dirty than who?

Cooke *(deer in headlights)*: Uh . . . Uh . . .

Campbell *(nonchalantly rolling up his sleeves)*: Everyone leave the room, please.

Murphy sprints for the door. Dr. Mellieux leaves his chair spinning, while Bettman leaps over the table. The pizza delivery guy struggles to commando-crawl out the door, which is then quickly slammed and padlocked shut. The group huddles fearfully in the hallway for several moments.

Campbell *(from inside the room)*: Incoming!

An airborne Matt Cooke smashes through the window and lands in the hallway. Campbell steps through the broken glass and pauses over Cooke's dazed body.

Campbell *(dusting himself off)*: When he comes to, tell him he's done until the second round of the playoffs. After all, we have to send a message that there are certain lines that just can't be crossed.

A COMPLETE
TRANSCRIPT OF
EVERY POST-GAME
CALL-IN SHOW EVER
BROADCAST

Host: Hello, everyone, and welcome to tonight's broadcast of every post-game call-in show ever. I'm your host, the lowest-ranking employee of this station. I will now read the phone number too quickly for anyone to write down because I'm hoping against hope that we have no callers tonight. Let's go to the phones!

Caller #1: Yes, hi. I have an opinion on the game I just listened to that will make it abundantly clear that I lack even a basic understanding of hockey.

Host: I will attempt to politely correct your misconceptions while letting the tone of my voice imply that you are a simpleton.

Caller #1: This is a counterpoint that is based on a strategy I once used in *NHL 94*.

Host: I will now hang up on you but pretend it was your cell phone malfunctioning. Next caller?

Caller #2: I'd like to waste airtime by informing you of how long I've been a listener.

Host: I am sounding mildly annoyed while I say thanks and urge you to go ahead.

Caller #2: This is a generic observation about tonight's game, which is technically accurate but so breathtakingly obvious as to be completely worthless.

Host: I am sitting with my eyes closed and quietly rubbing my temples while I throw to the next caller.

Caller #3: The previous caller made the exact same point I wanted to make, but I will repeat it instead of just hanging up, because I like the sound of my own voice.

Host: Duly noted. Next caller, hello?

Caller #4: I am confused because I'm trying to listen to myself on the radio while I talk to you.

Host: Have you not listened to a call-in program in the last thirty years, caller?

Caller #4 (*echoing faintly*): WHAT IS HAPPENING?

Host: Well, at least this can't get any worse. Next caller?

Caller #5: I have a trade proposal.

Host: Oh dear lord.

Caller #5: Here is my completely ridiculous proposal, which involves acquiring a superstar player from another team in exchange for several terrible players and, to make it fair, a fourth-round pick.

Host: I am unscrewing the top on a bottle of Jack Daniel's while awaiting your explanation of why any team would want to trade a superstar for a collection of players that fans in this city have concluded are terrible.

Caller #5: I am basing my proposal on the assumption that the other team will be unaware of this, as they do not employ any scouts or have access to a television.

Host: I am trying but failing to disguise the disgust in my voice as I throw to the next caller.

Caller #6: I am reading this overly scripted call from a piece of paper while trying very hard to sound like Jim Rome.

Host: I am regretting every vocational decision I have ever made.

Caller #6: Failed attempt to introduce my own catch-phrase.

Host: Next caller.

Caller #7: I have a surprisingly rational and well-reasoned point to make that is critical of senior members of the team's front office.

Host: I am afraid to say anything because we are the official radio rights holder and cannot criticize the team in any meaningful way.

Caller #7: Continued cogent argument.

Host: Cell phone malfunction!

Caller #7: *(dial tone)*

Host: I see that it's now time for my producer to awkwardly get his nightly seven seconds of airtime for no reason.

Producer: My voice is disturbingly squeaky.

Host: Back to the callers!

Caller #8: I would like to explain an elaborate league-wide conspiracy theory, based on one icing call that went against my team in the first period.

Host: I will allow you to continue talking because I am furiously updating my résumé.

Caller #8: I will continue explaining the vast officiating conspiracy against my team while ignoring the fact that our best player broke his stick over the referee's head without receiving a penalty in both the second and third periods.

Host: I will now try to fit in one last caller even though we are seven seconds away from having to go to a break.

Caller #9: Why are you playing music over top of . . .

Host: Sorry, caller, we need to go. Stay tuned for a sports update that will tell you the score of a game we just spent twenty minutes talking about, followed by three dozen used car commercials, followed by me crying silently into the microphone until morning.

DEAR SON, WELCOME TO LIFE AS A TORONTO MAPLE LEAFS FAN

In the summer of 2010, my wife and I welcomed our first son into the world. Like any proud father, I didn't want to waste any time teaching him the important values that I hope he'll carry with him throughout his life. So as soon as he was old enough, I sat him down for a very important discussion.

Hey, little guy. Wakey wakey. Daddy wants to share something very important with you.

Do you see this friendly-looking blue thing right here? That's a Toronto Maple Leafs logo. It probably looks familiar, since there's at least one on every item of clothing you own right now. And that's because you're going to be a Maple Leafs fan, just like your dad.

I want to tell you all about the Leafs. I want to teach you about Dave Keon and Borje Salming and Mats Sundin and

Teeder Kennedy. So let's look through Daddy's old scrapbook together, and I'll tell you all about them.

Look, here's a picture of George Armstrong. He was called "Chief." He's scoring the clinching goal into an empty net to beat the Montreal Canadiens. Look how happy everyone looks! Do you see all the people cheering? They're happy because they just saw the Leafs win their most recent Stanley Cup.

What's that? No. No, there aren't any pictures of this that are in color.

Because they didn't have color photography back in 1967, that's why. Well I'm sorry, that's just the way it is. Look, if you want to see them in color so badly, go ask your sister if you can borrow her crayons.

Hey, come on now, little buddy, stop crying.

It's not like Leafs fans haven't had anything to cheer about since then. Let me tell you about 1993. That's the year that the Leafs went on a magical run and almost made the Stanley Cup final. They had Dougie Gilmour's spinorama and Felix Potvin's brilliance and Wendel Clark punched out Marty McSorley's eyeball. It was probably the greatest stretch of hockey I've ever seen.

Yes, that's right, 1993.

Well of course that seems like a long time ago to you, you're a baby. Right, OK, I guess that was almost twenty years ago, sure. Nice math skills, Archimedes, do you have a point?

I said stop crying!

Look, I never said being a Leafs fan was going to be easy, OK? But I'm not raising you to be some sort of front-running bandwagon jumper who elbows his way to the head of the line when the team is winning and then bails out as soon as times get tough. The world already has too many Senators fans.

No, you're going to stick this out until the bitter end, and here's why: It will be worth it some day.

If you don't believe me, ask a Chicago Blackhawks fan. They hadn't won a Stanley Cup since 1961, but then that all changed. For a few years they finished in last place just like the Leafs, but now they have a roster full of young stars that they drafted and their team is . . .

What? No. No, the Leafs can't just go out and do that too. Because they don't have any draft picks, that's why. Because they gave them all to another team, OK? I don't know, because it seemed like a good idea at the time!

No, Daddy is not crying. Hey, isn't there an episode of *The Backyardigans* you should be watching?

Look, kid. I know it seems hopeless. I know it even seems a little bit cruel to raise you as a Leafs fan. I know that whenever you see Daddy thinking about the Leafs he's making angry faces and muttering mean words and drinking from one of his special grown-up bottles.

But here's the thing, son: Someday, the Leafs are going to win the Stanley Cup. It won't happen this year, or the next, or even the one after that. But it will happen one day. And when that day arrives, all the near misses and the lost seasons and the jokes and the blown calls and the sleepless nights will just make it all that much sweeter.

When that moment comes, someday a very long time from now, you're going to appreciate it in a way that only a true fan can. Because you'll have earned it.

That's why you're going to be a Leafs fan, son, whether you like it or not. But if those nice folks from Children Services ask, you chose this of your own free will, OK?

Now let's go get you changed. I think somebody made a Toskala in his diaper.